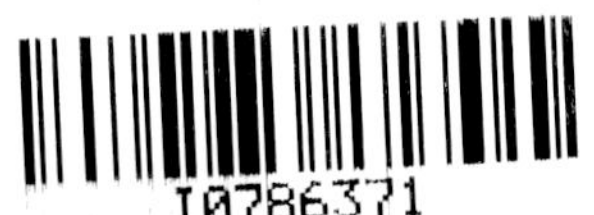

Kaleidoscope
Coloring Book

Copyright: Published in the United States by Peter Raymond
Published July 2018
ISBN-13: 978-1722273095
ISBN-10: 1722273097

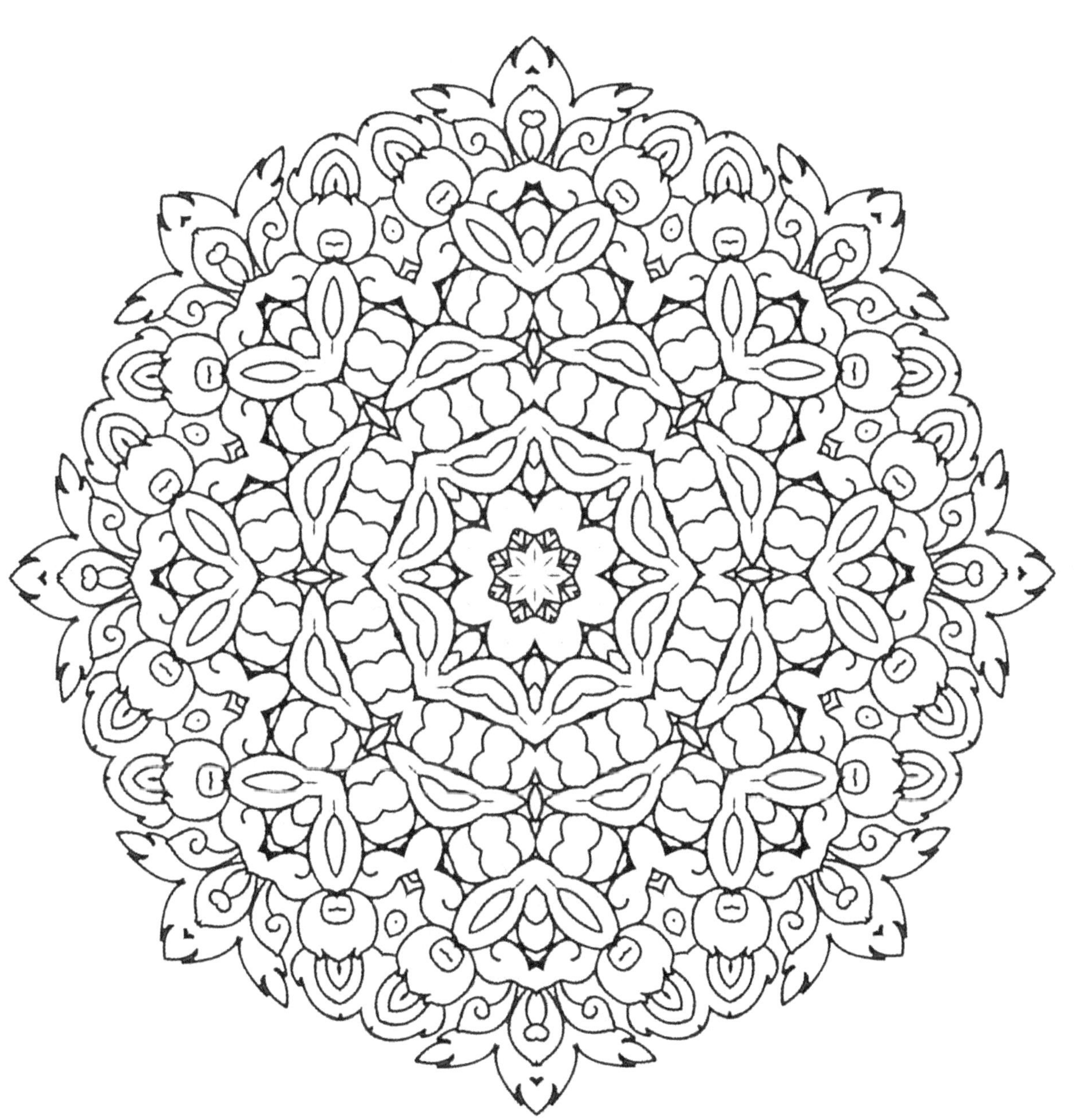

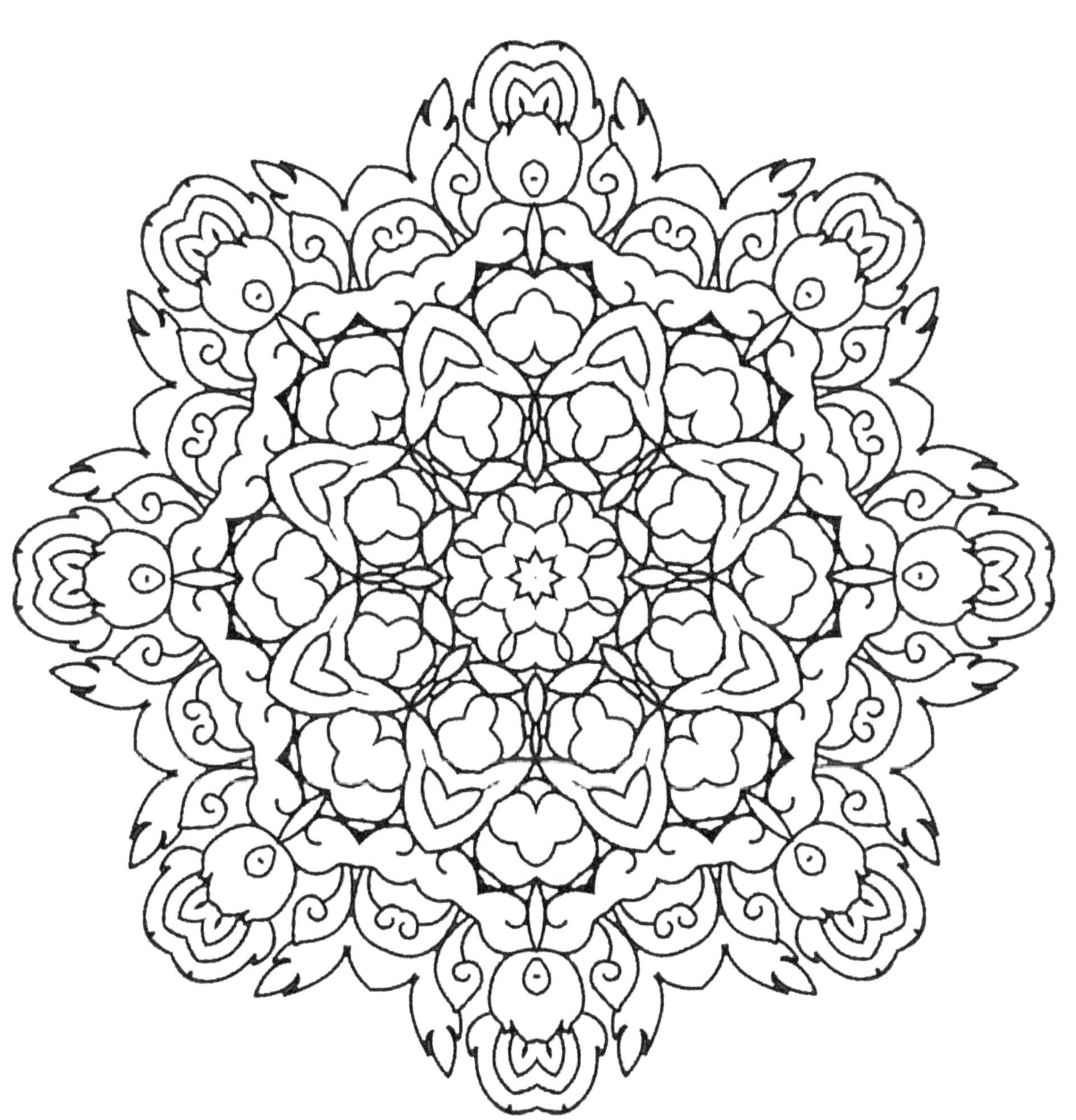

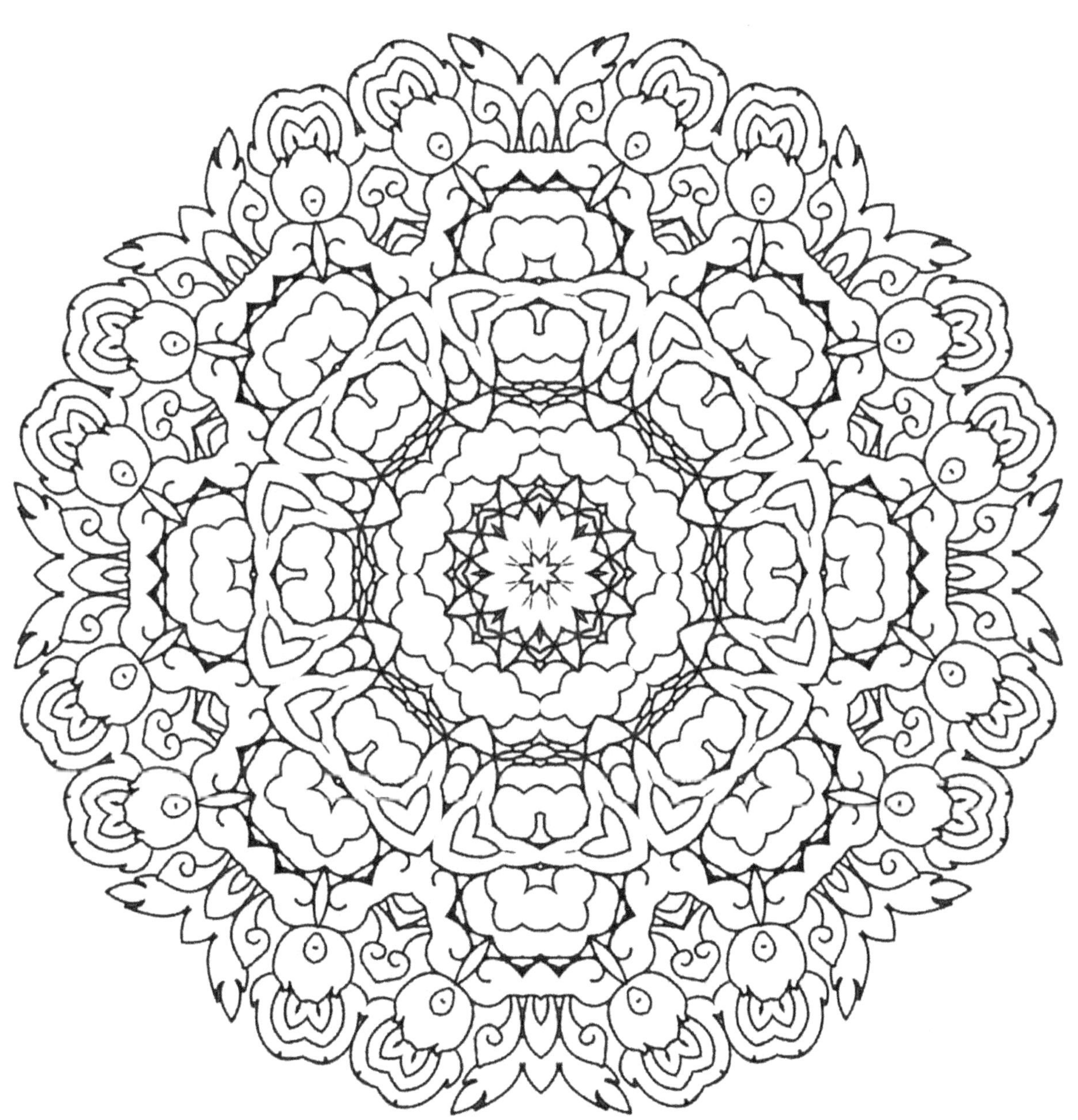

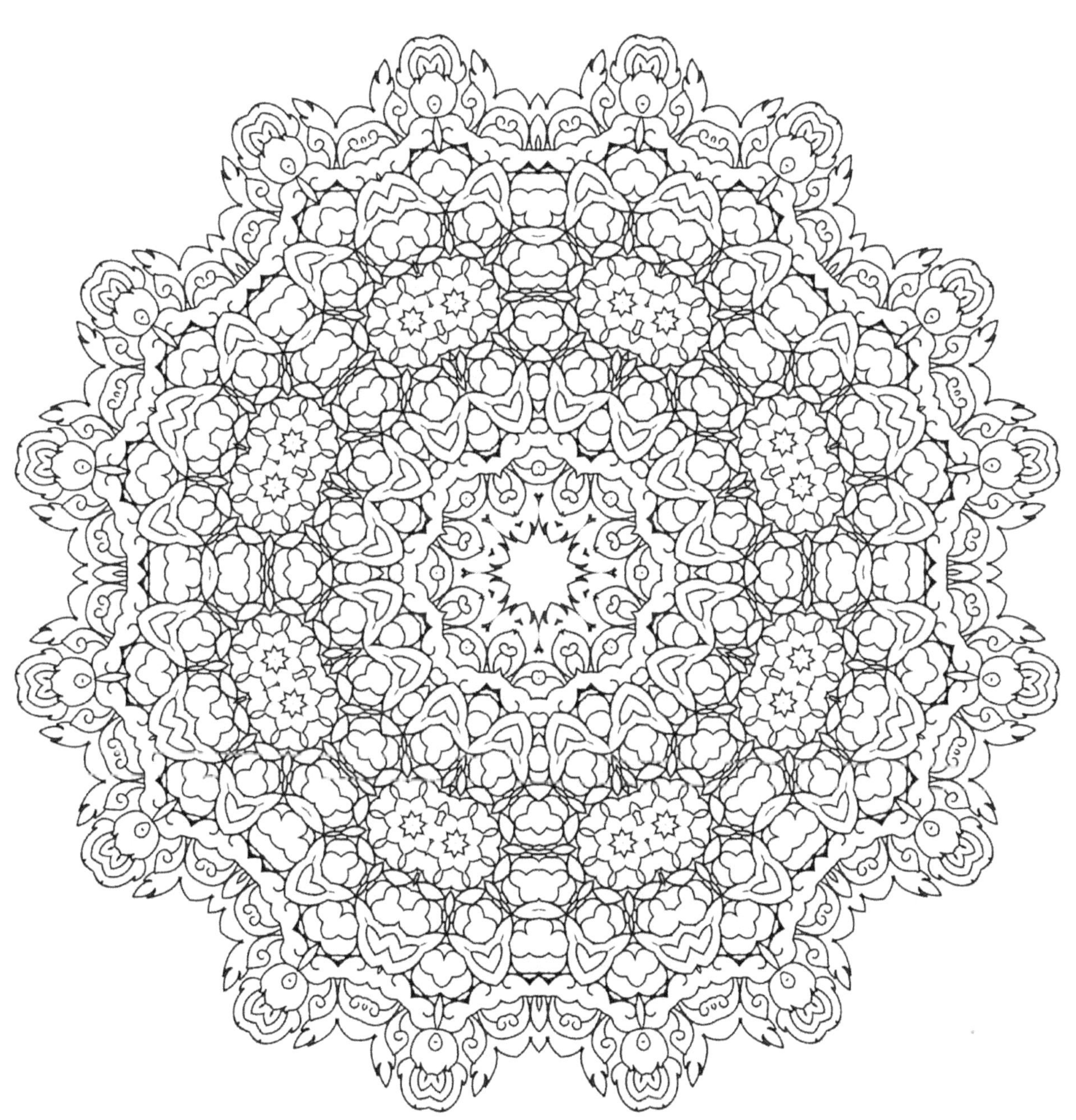

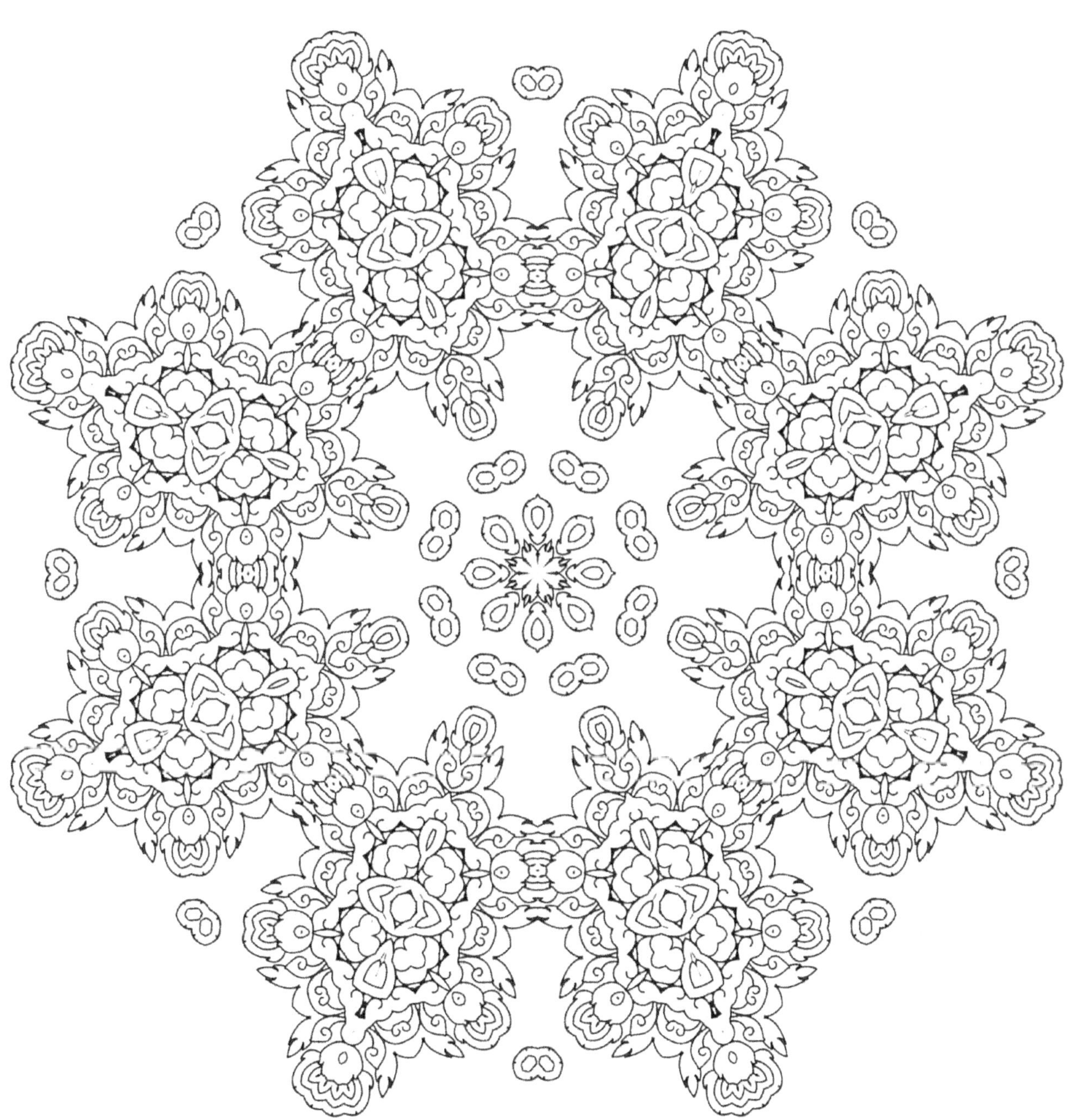

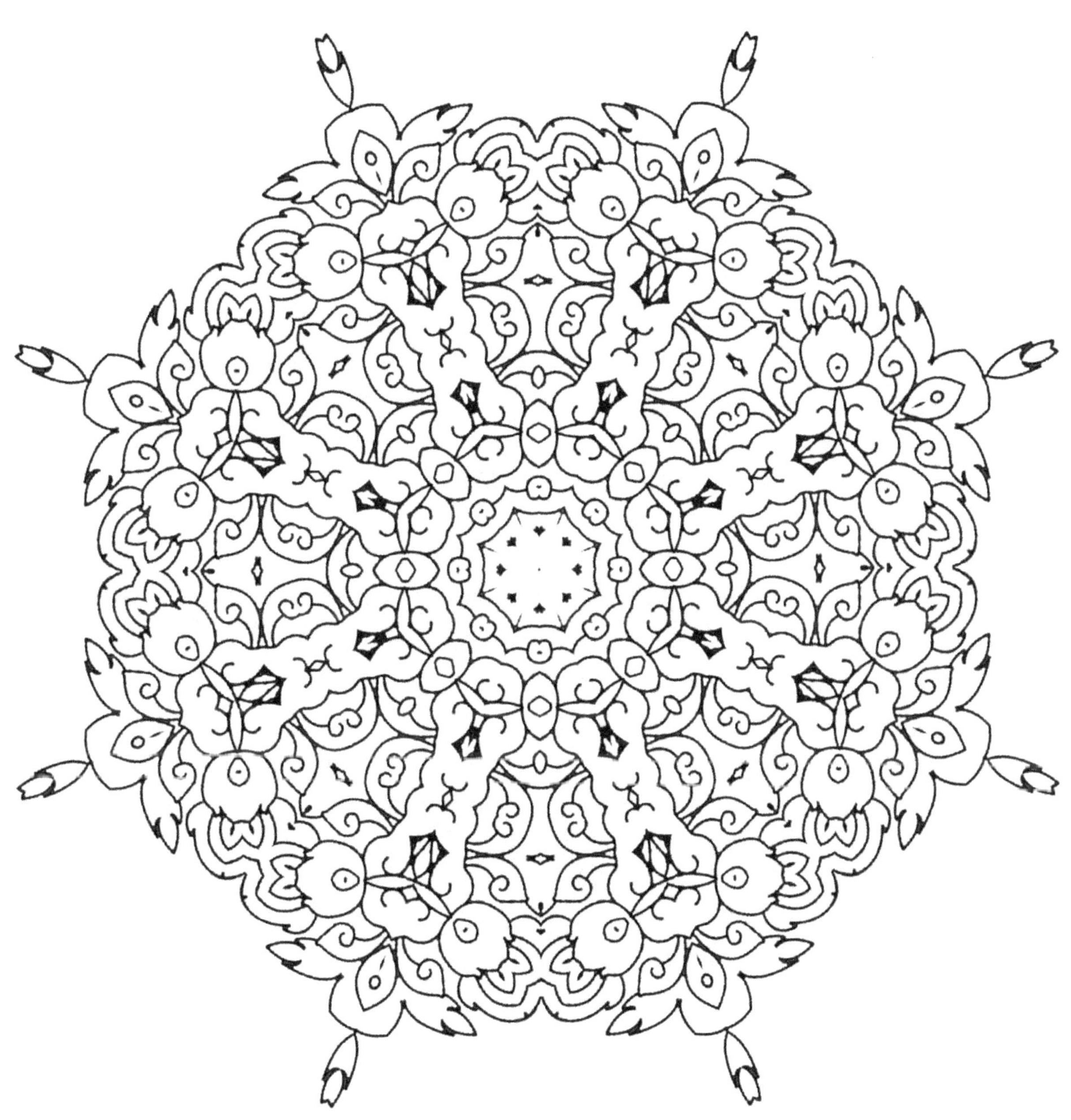

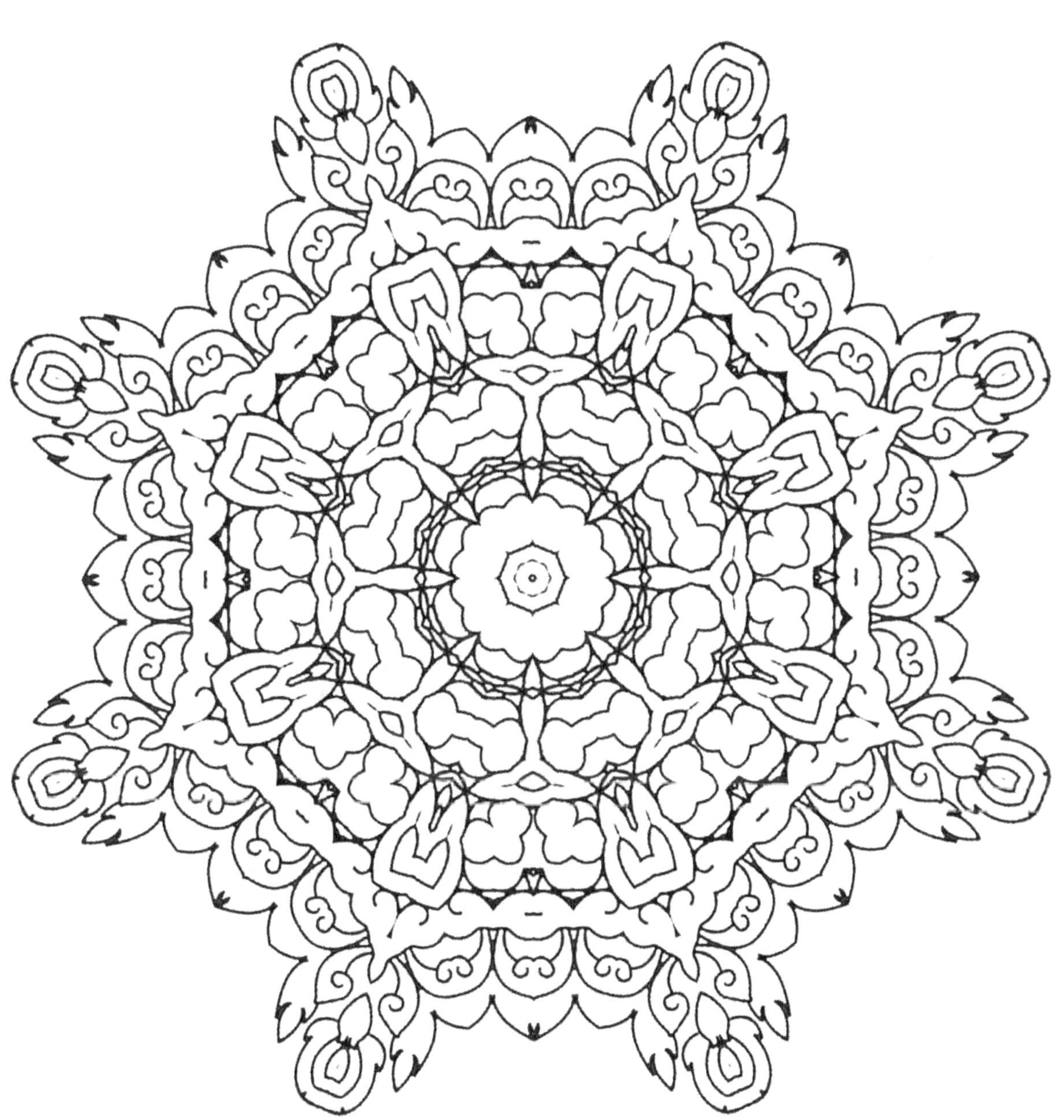

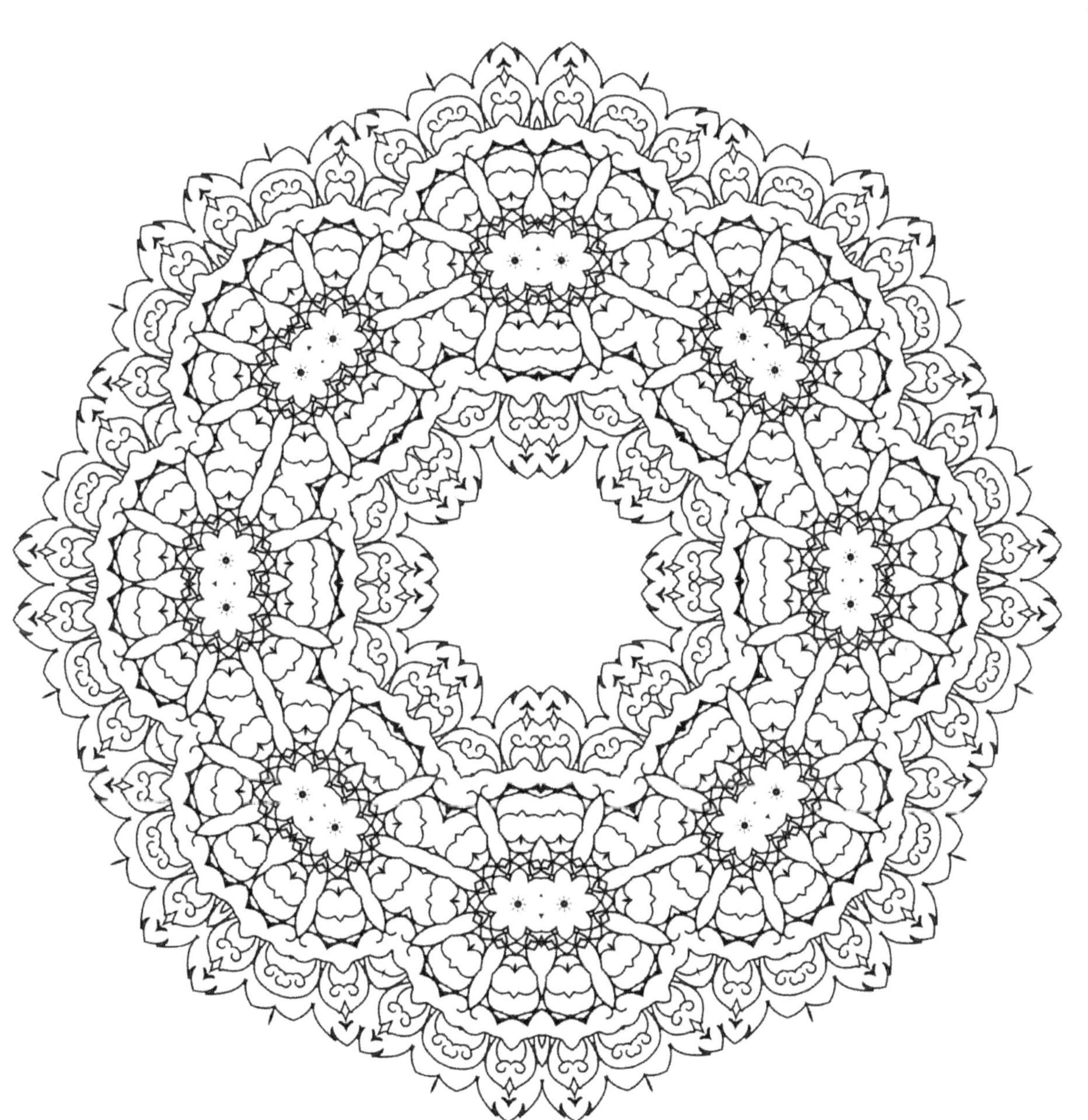

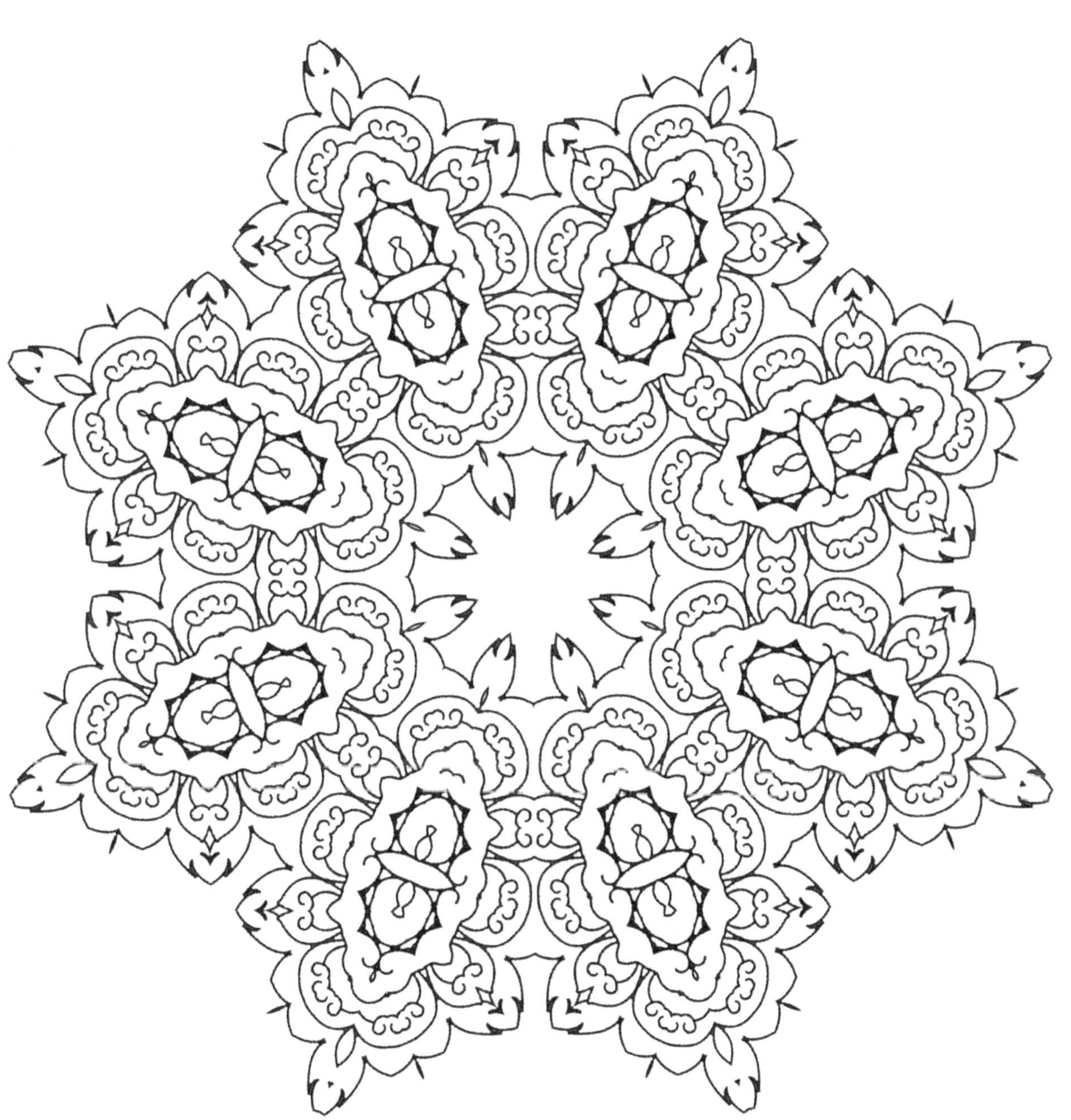

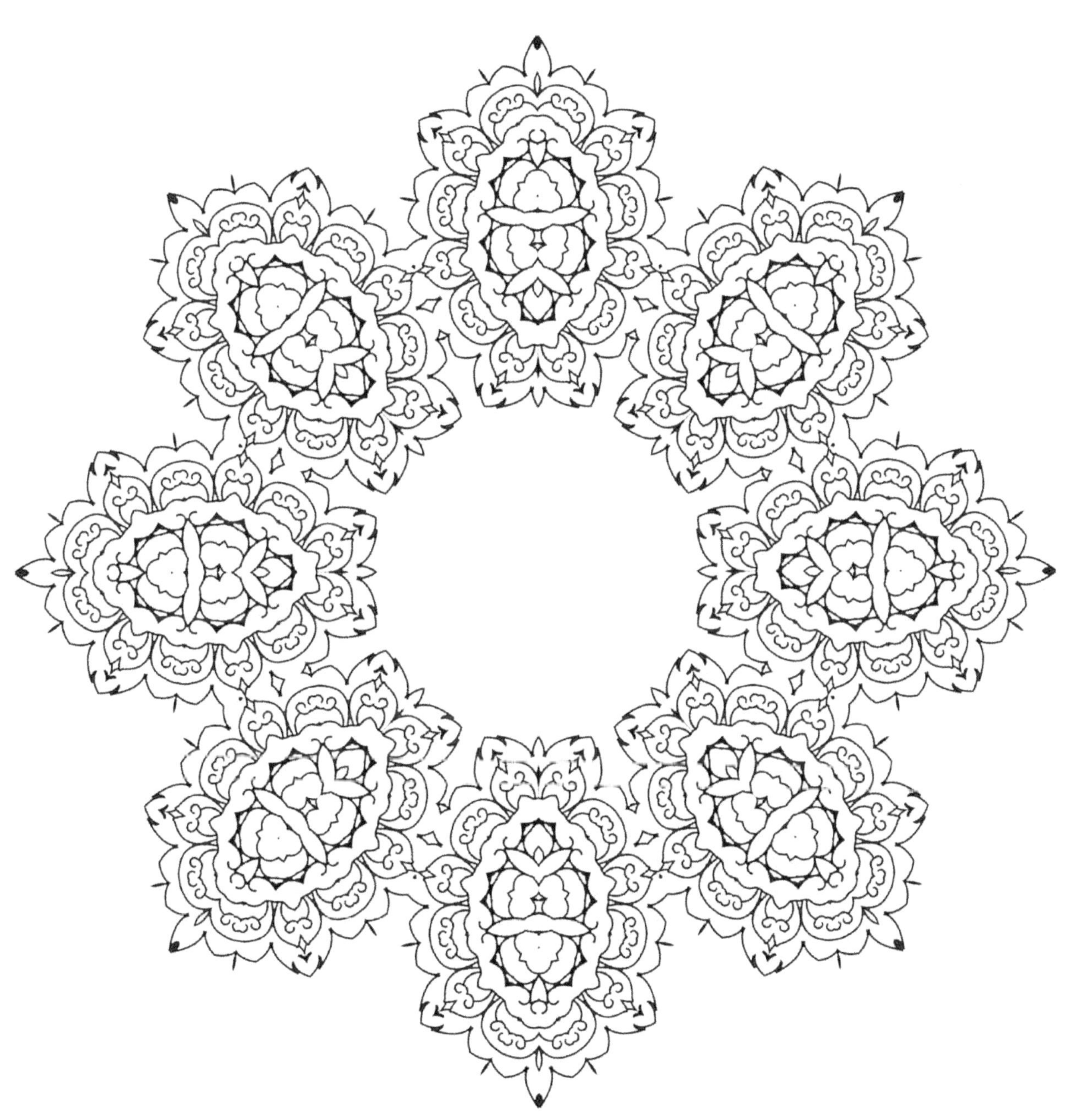

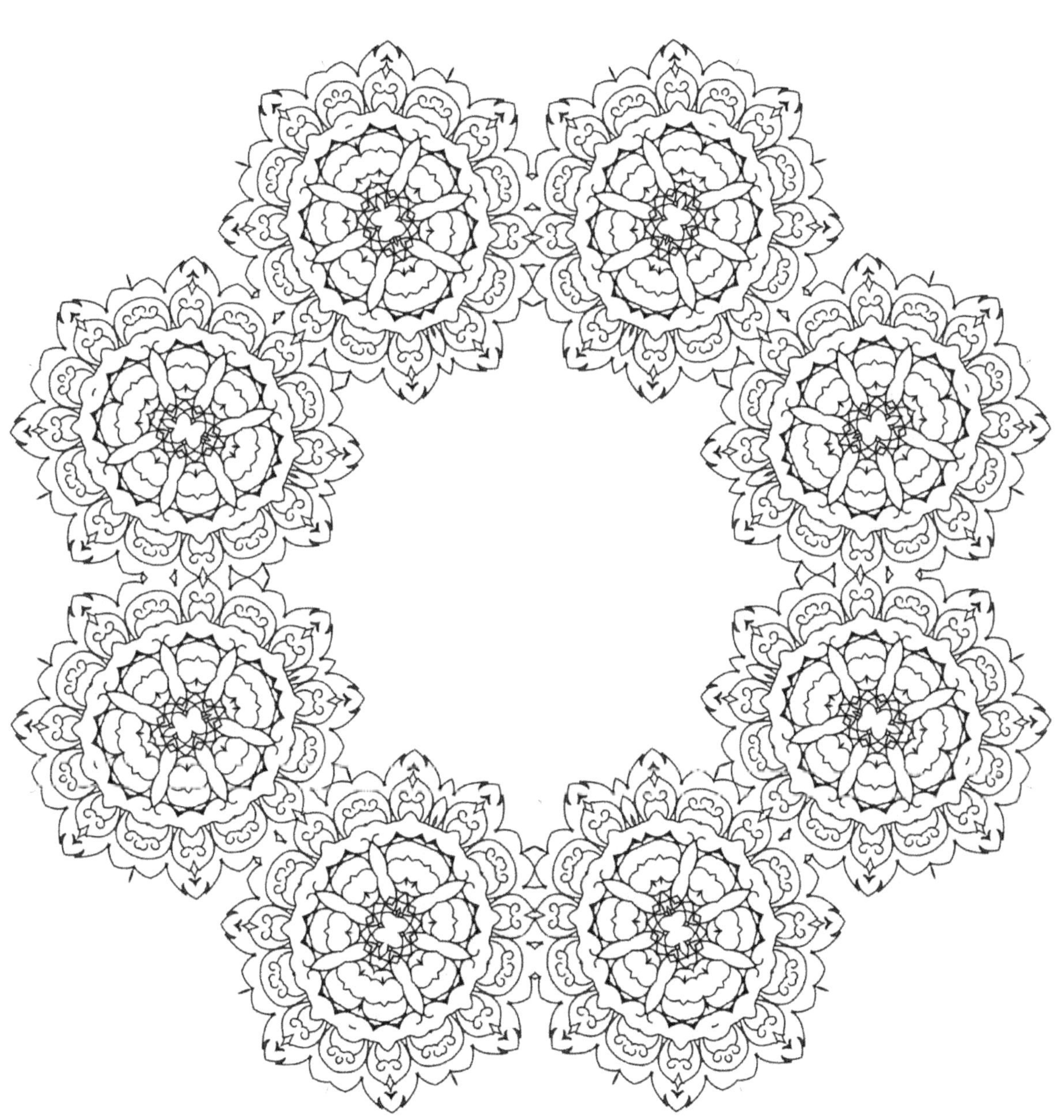

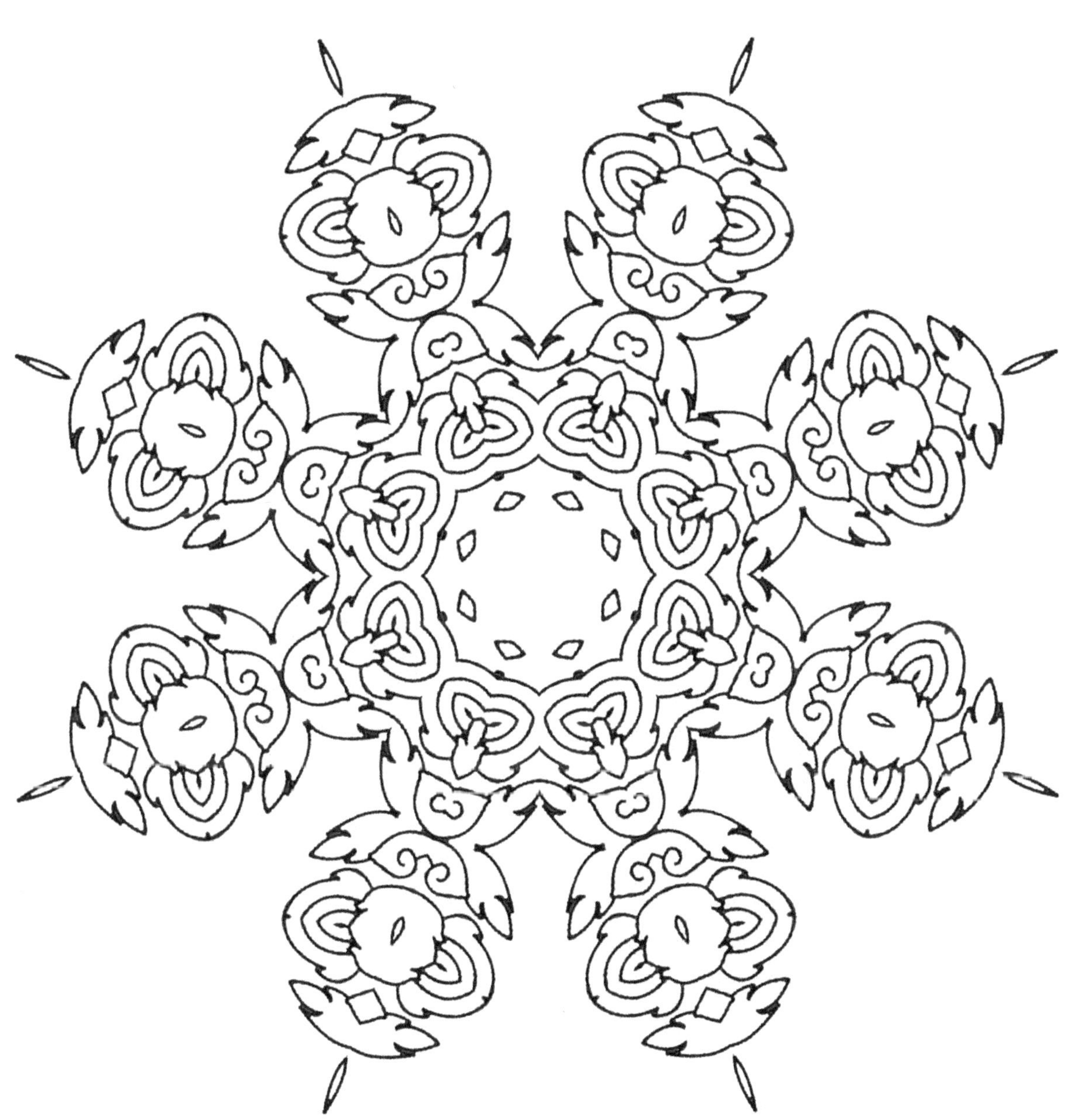

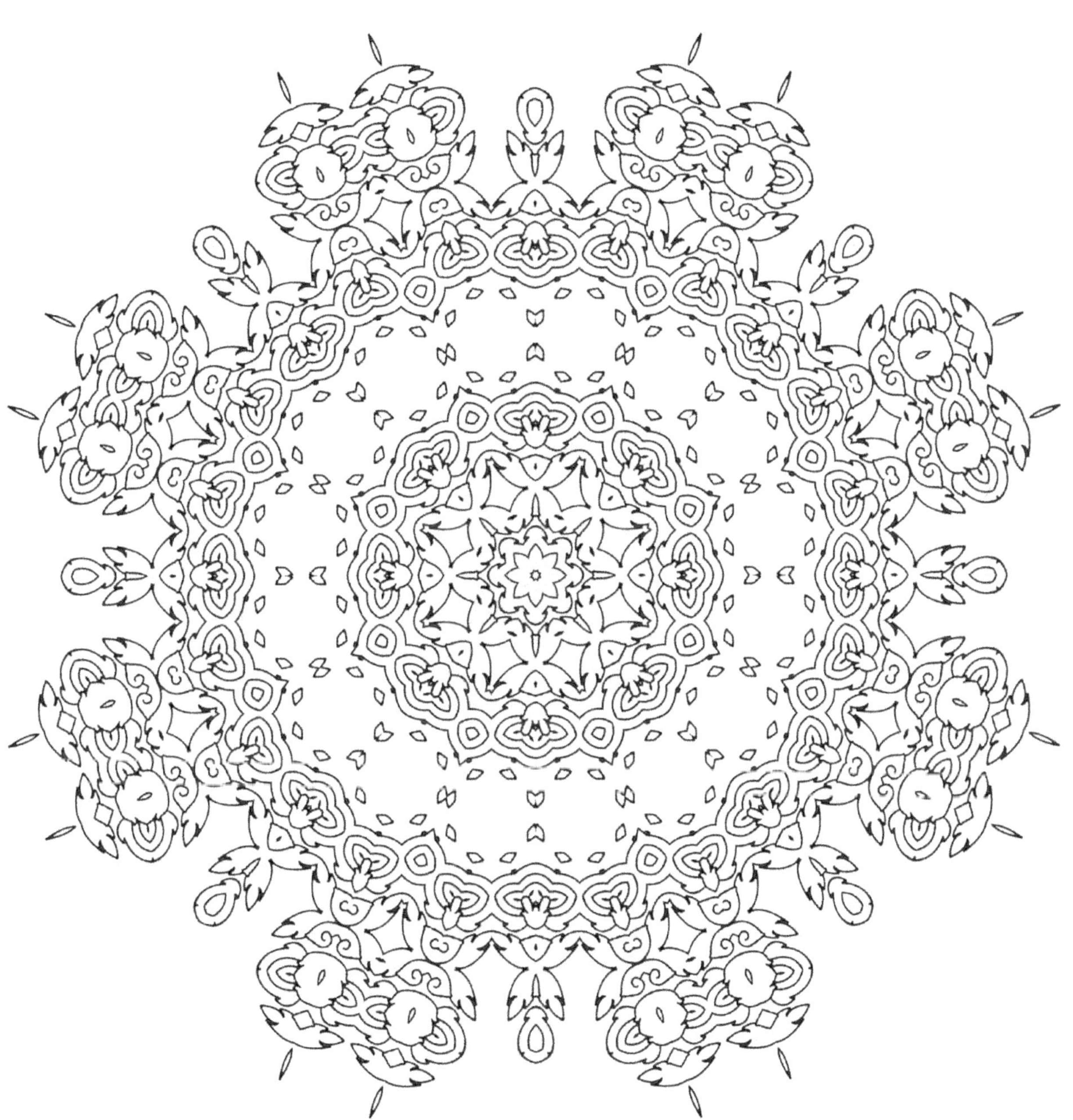

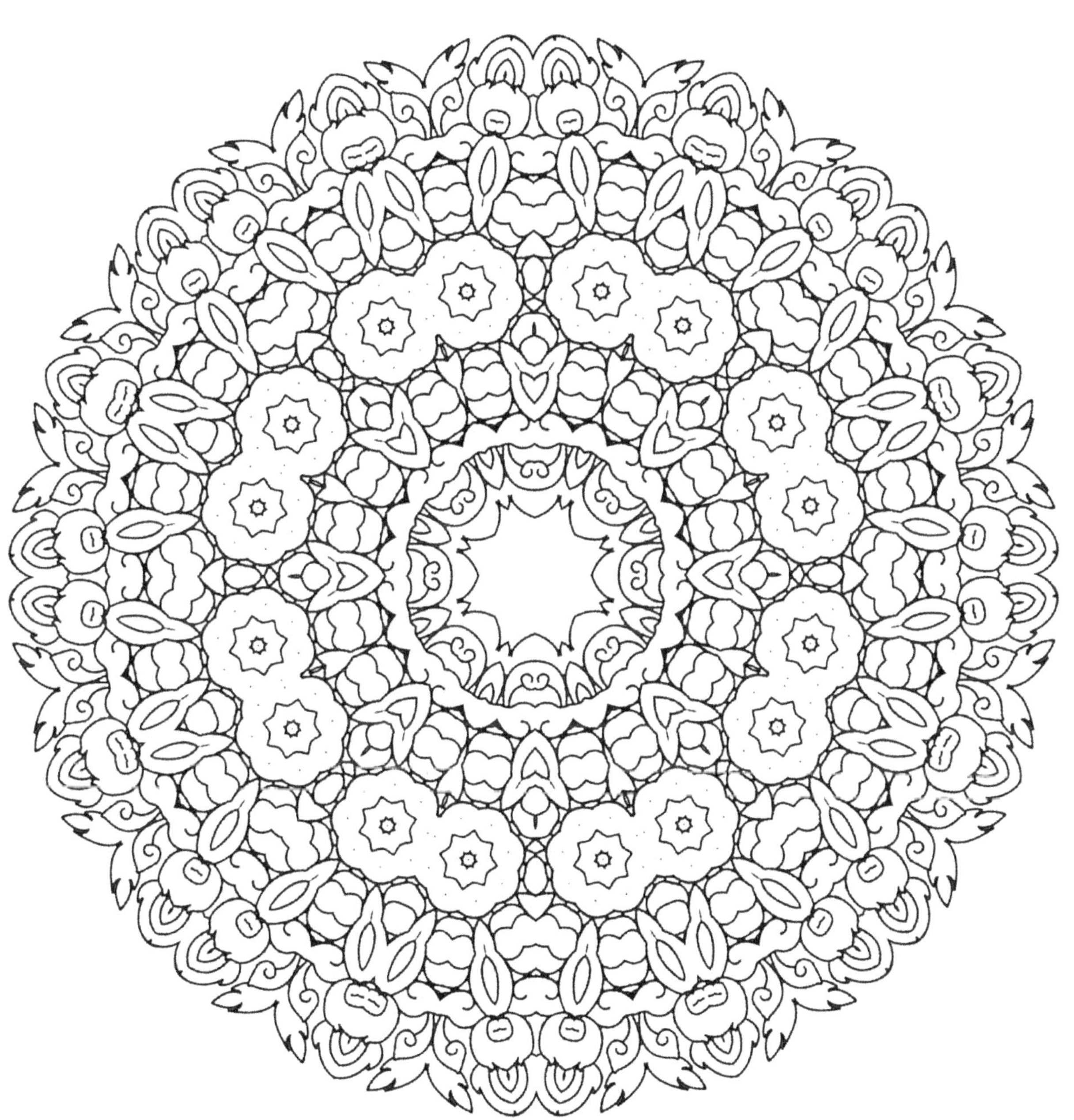

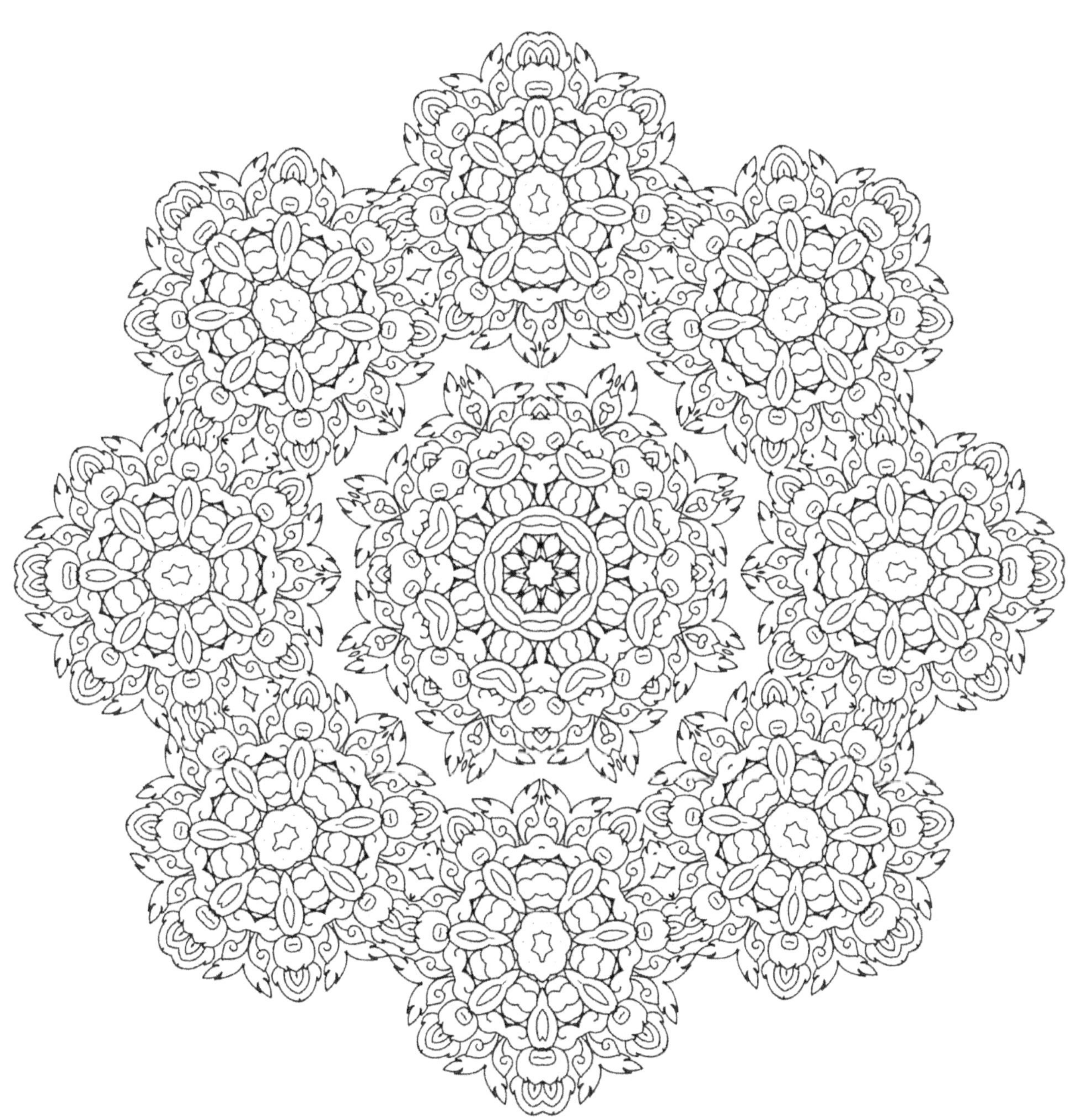

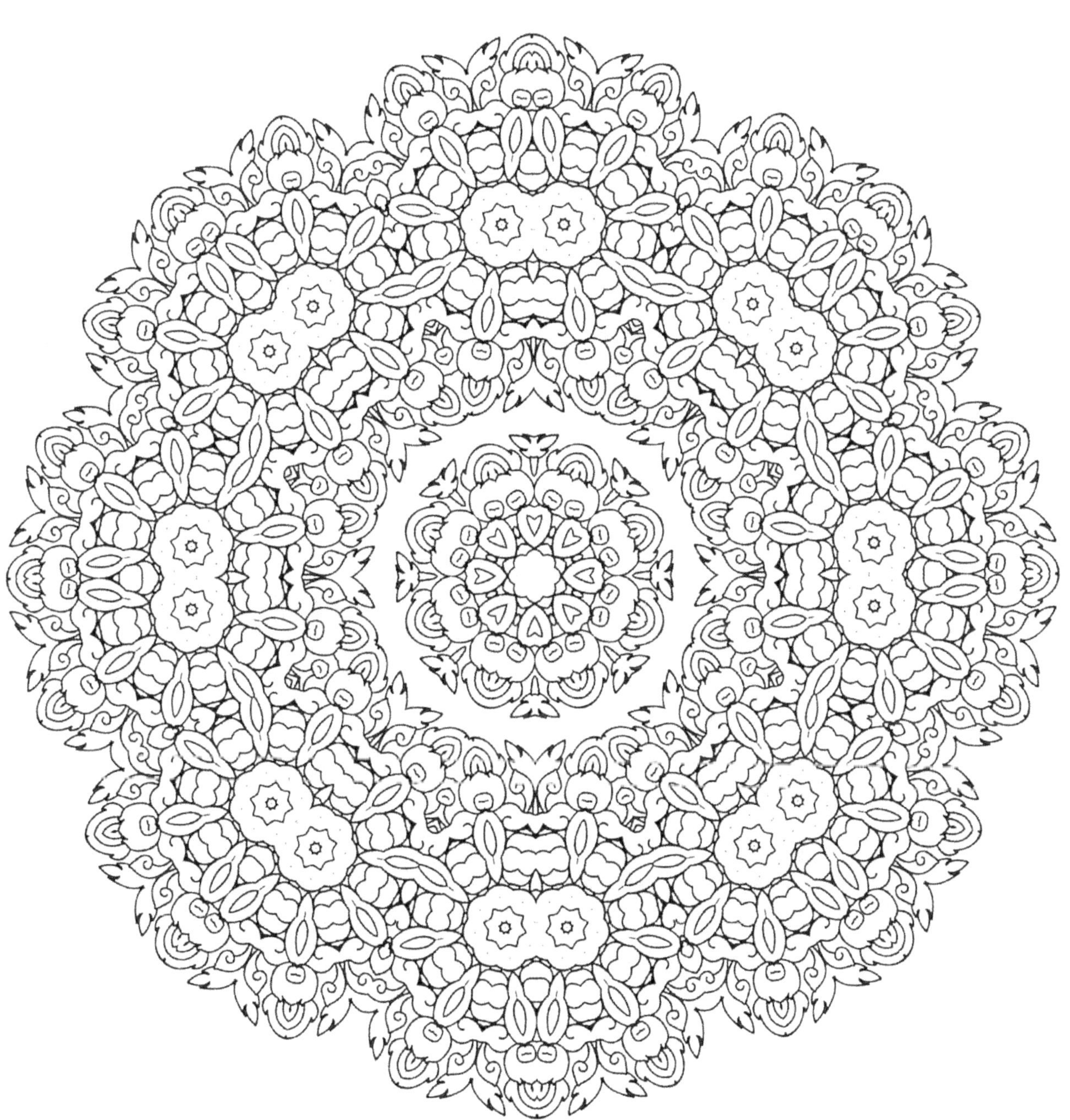

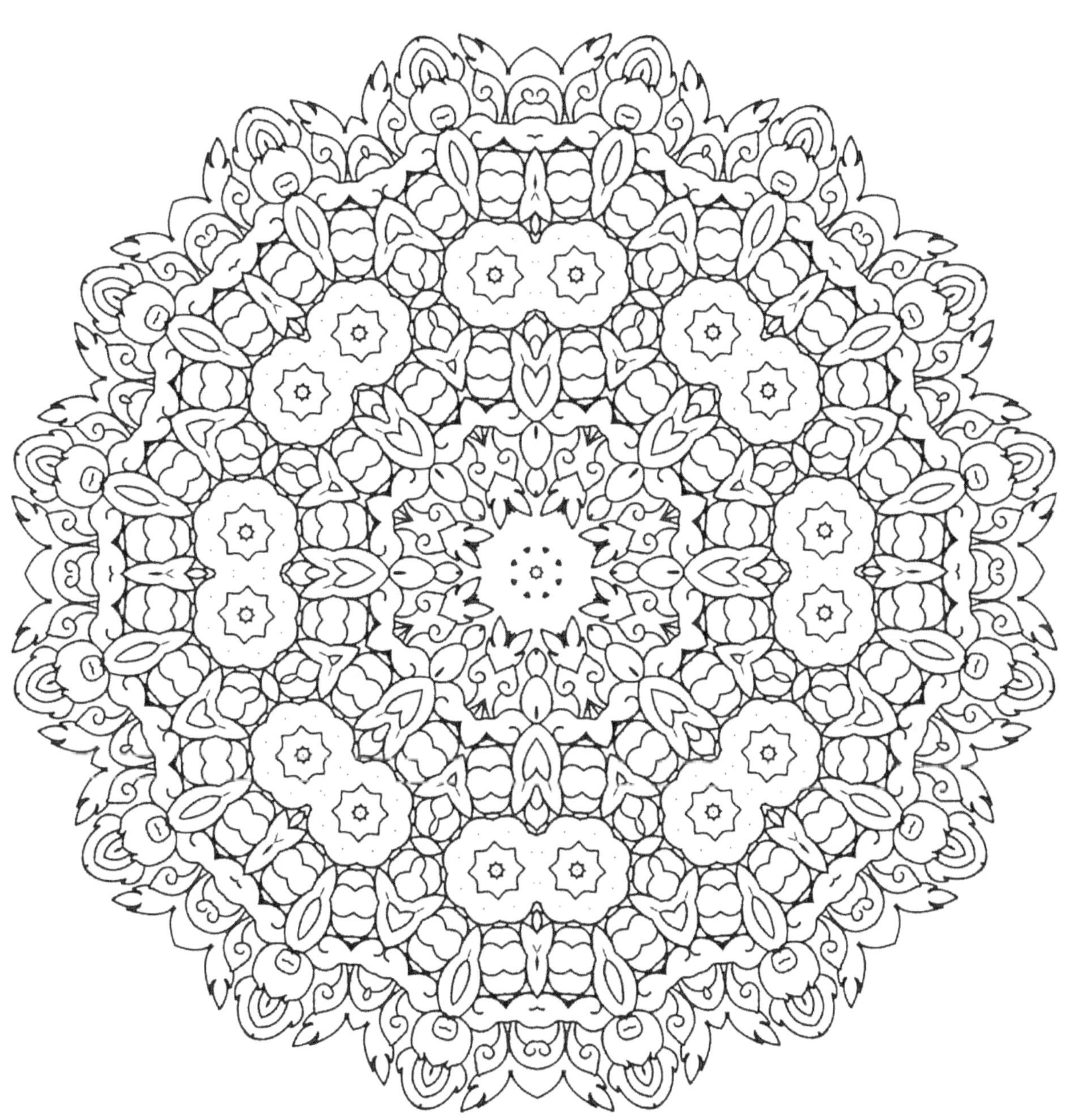

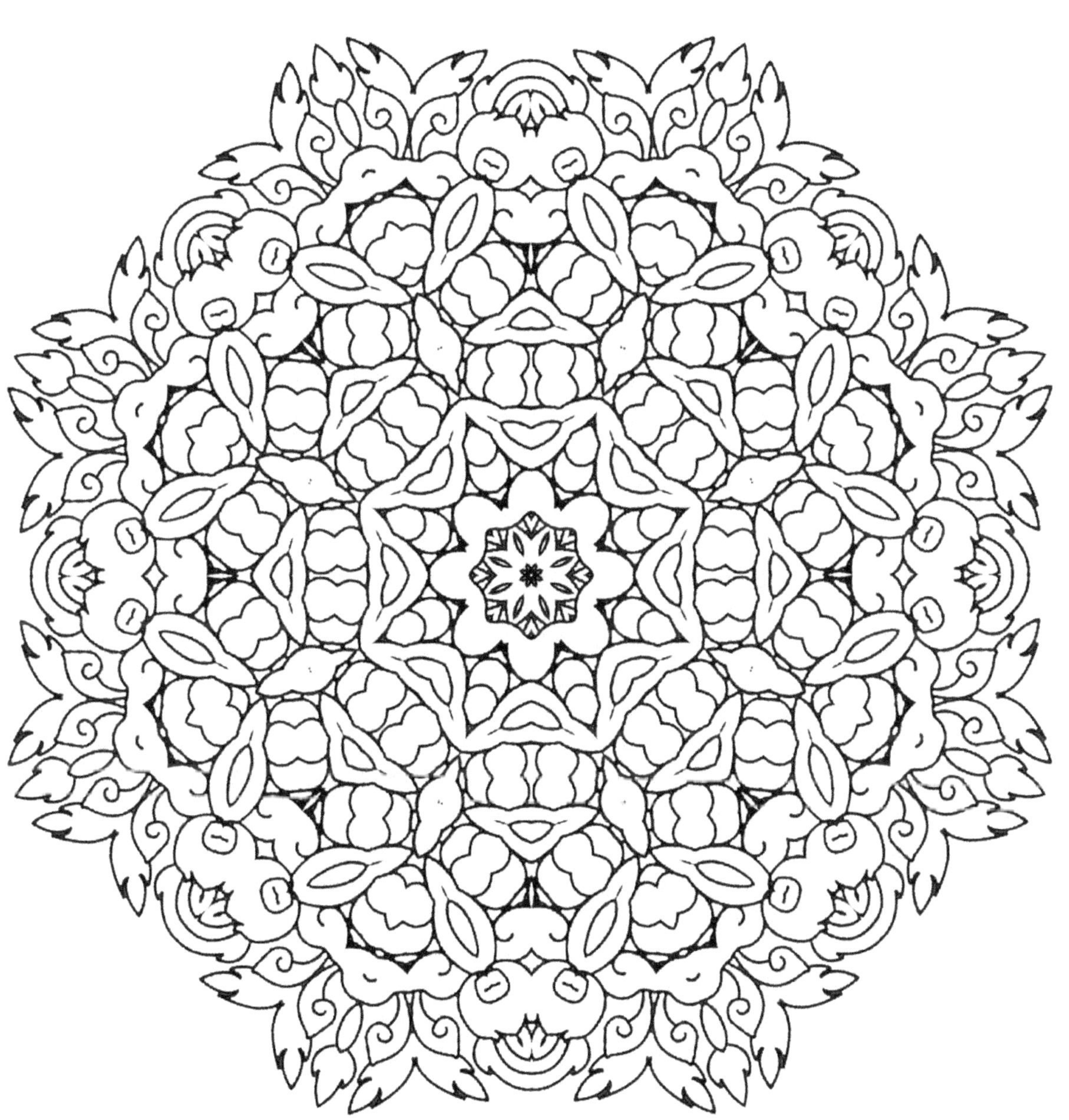

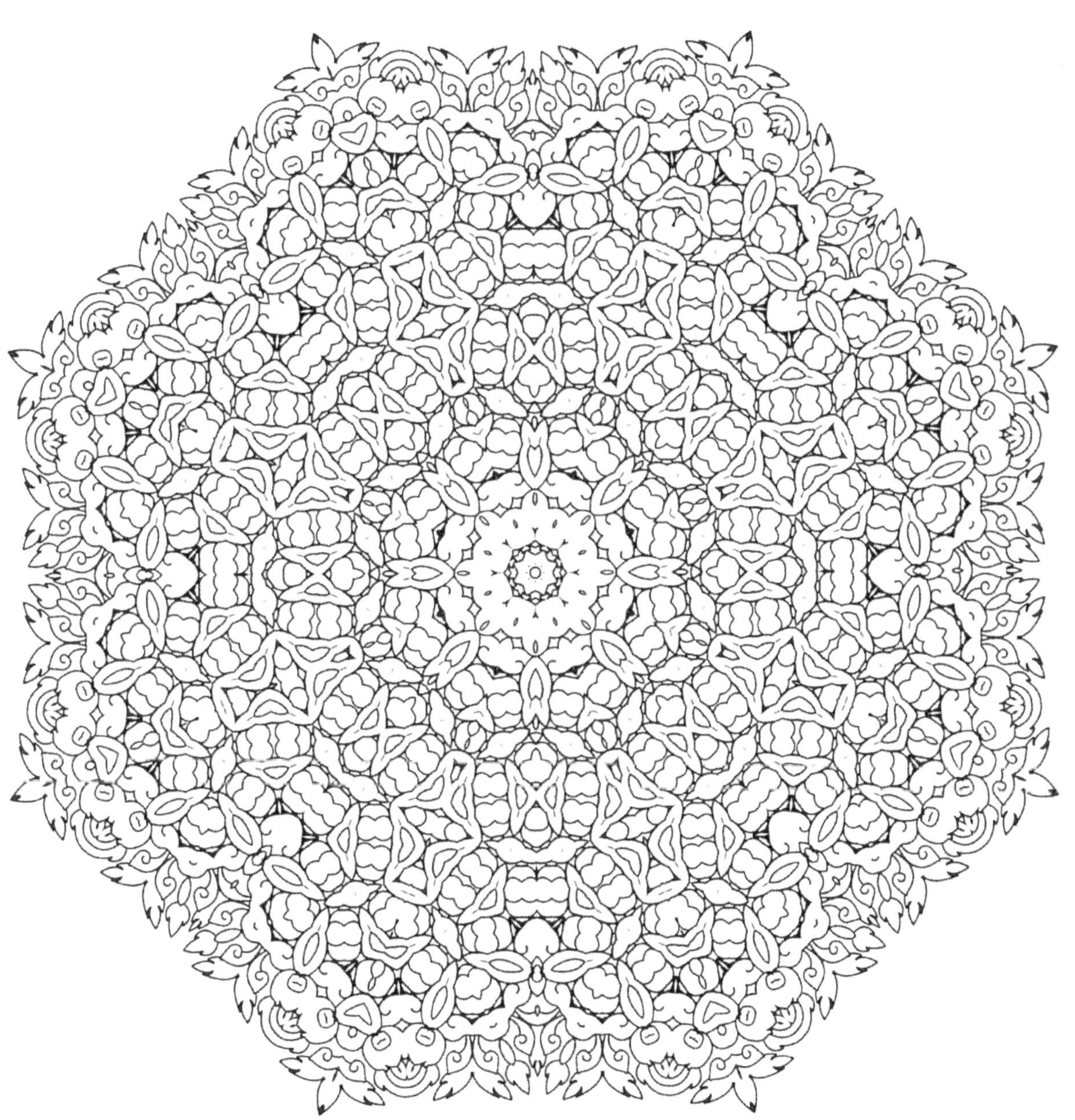

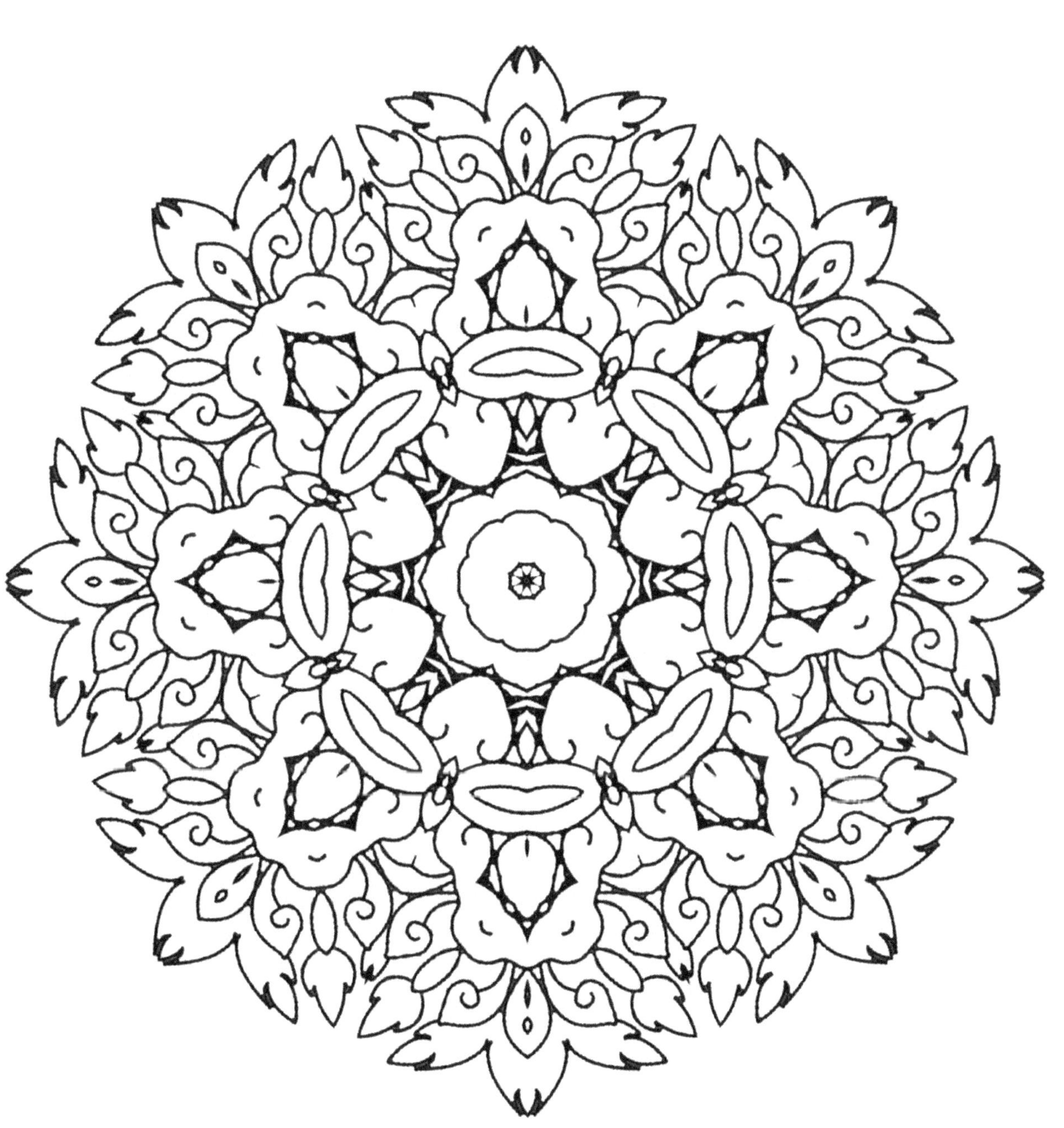

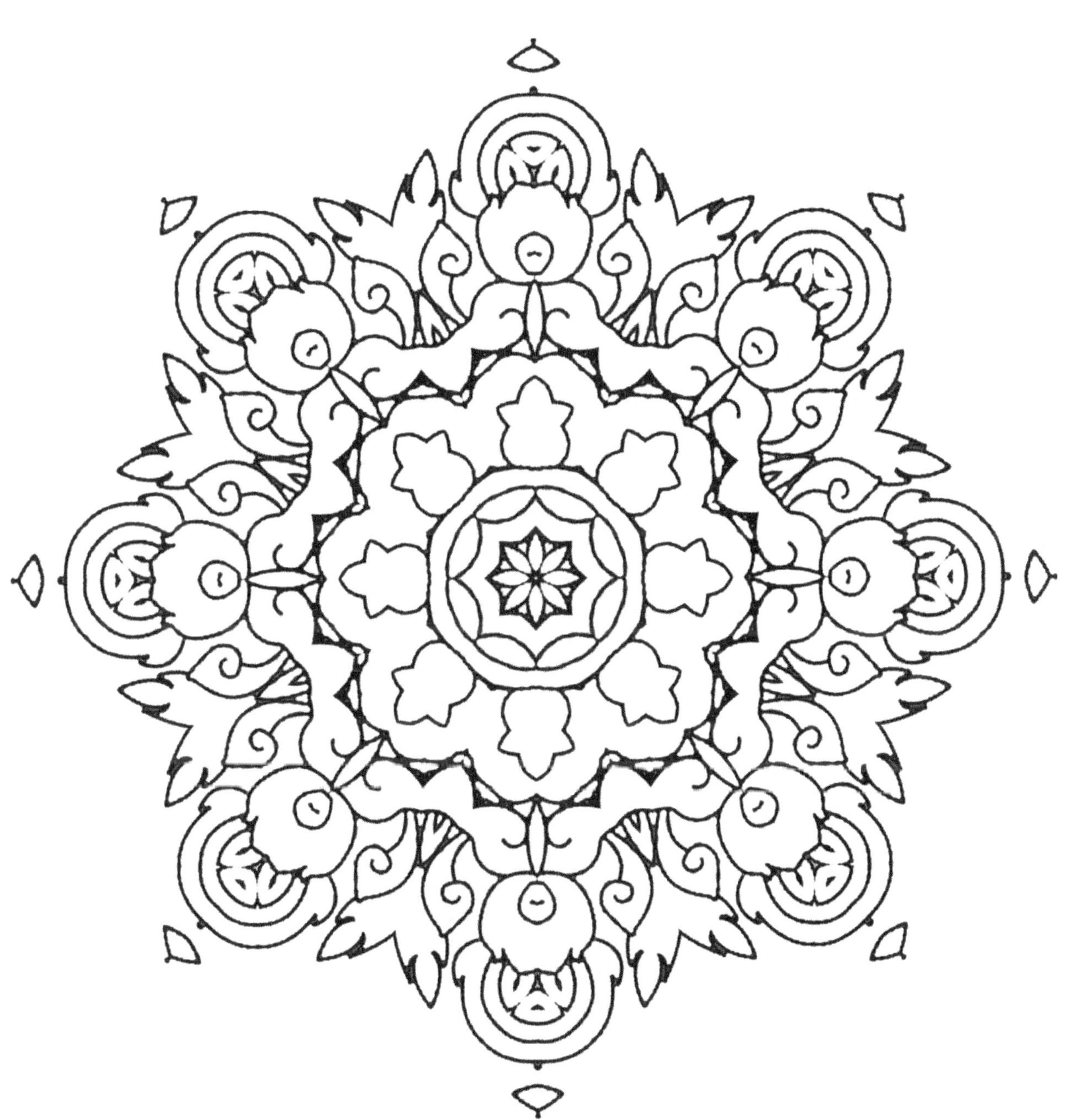

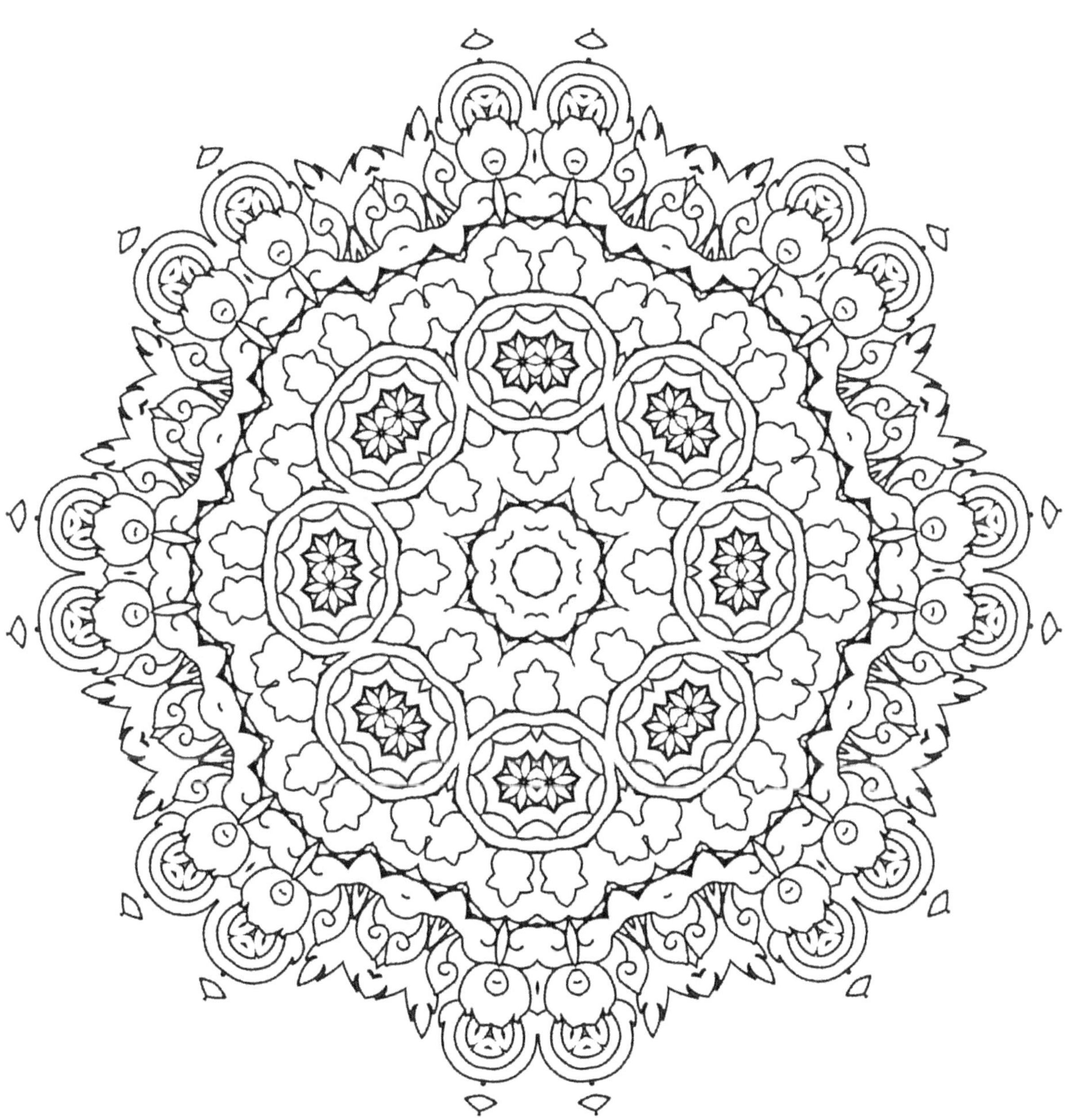

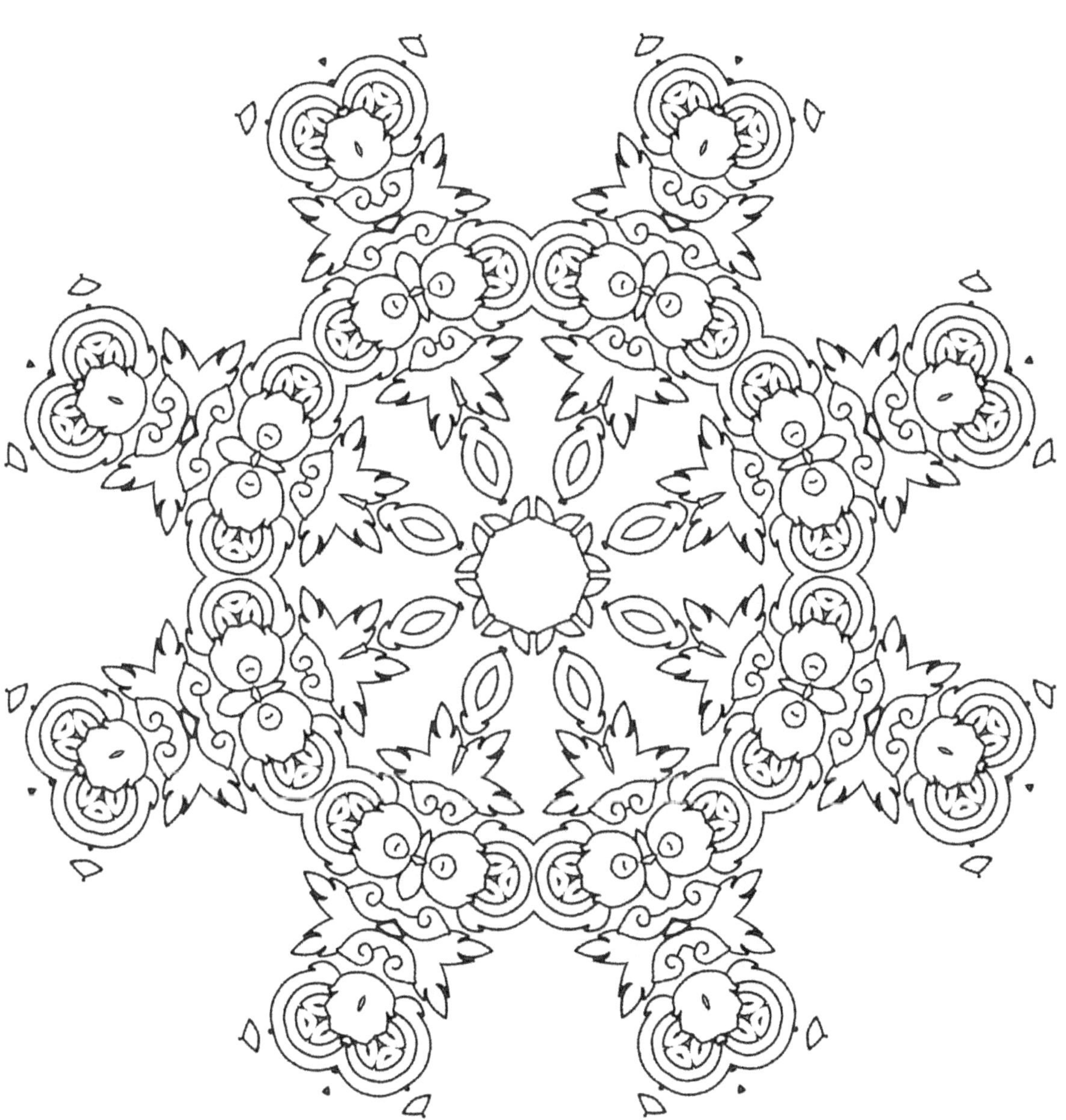

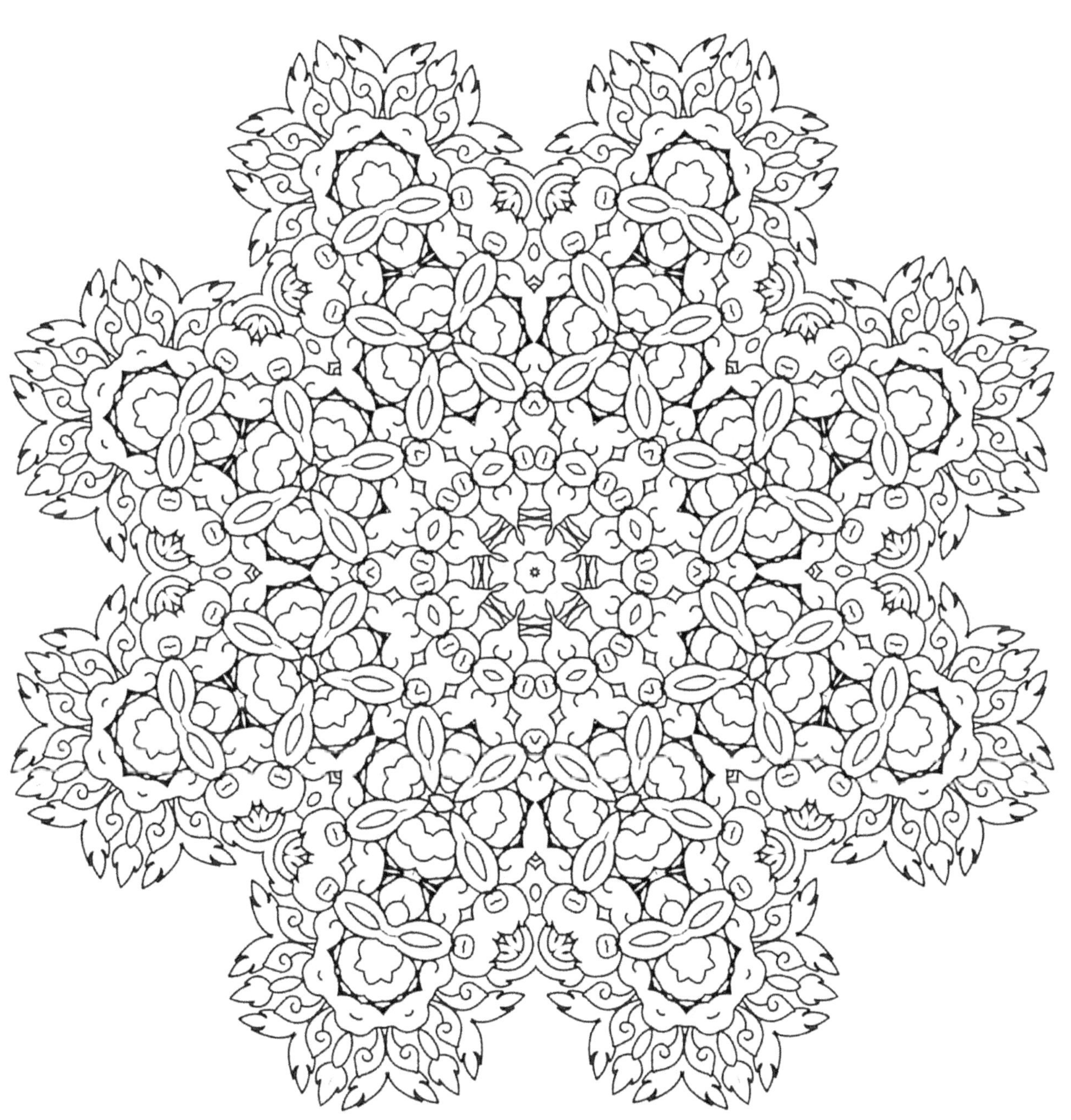

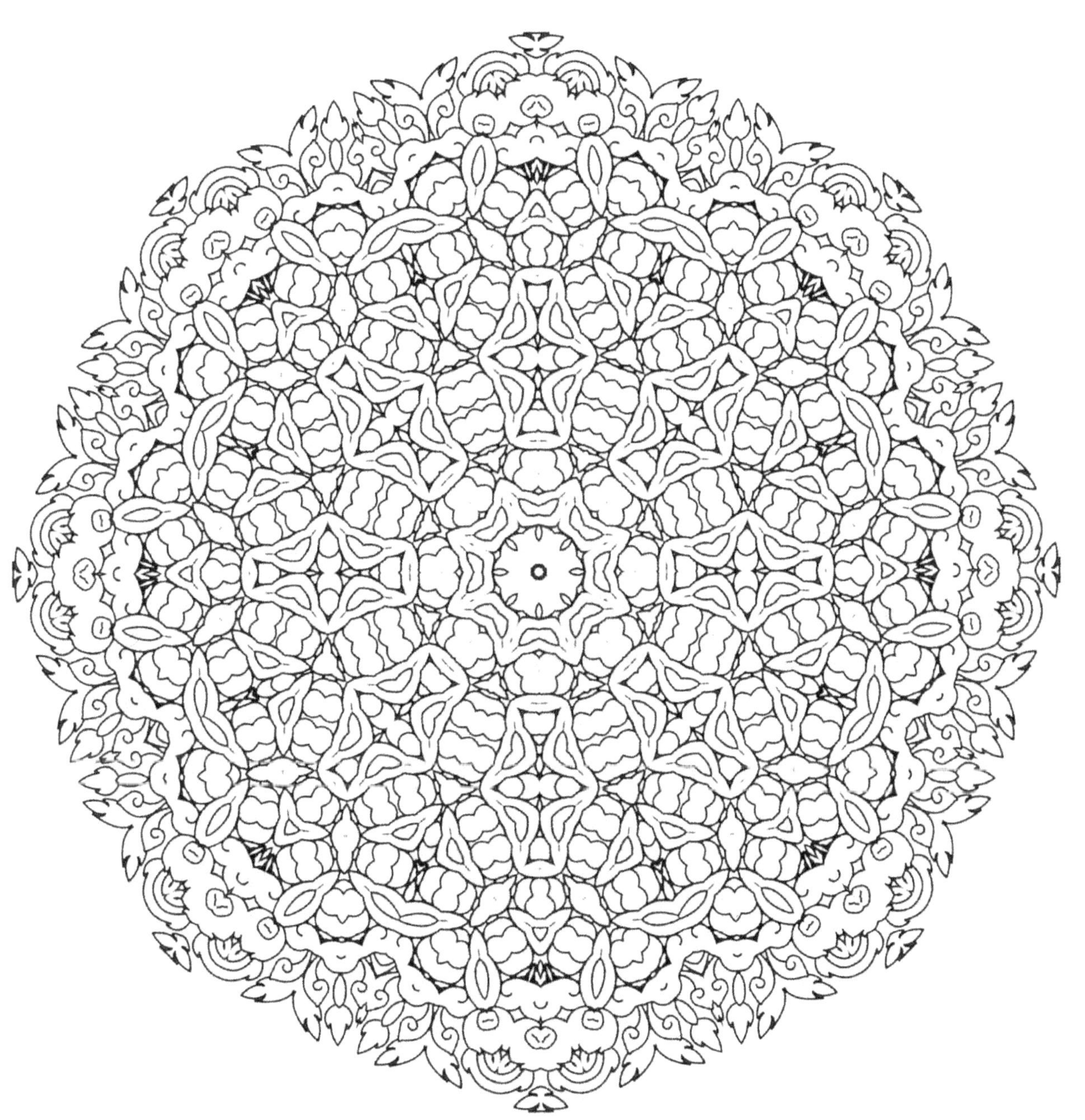

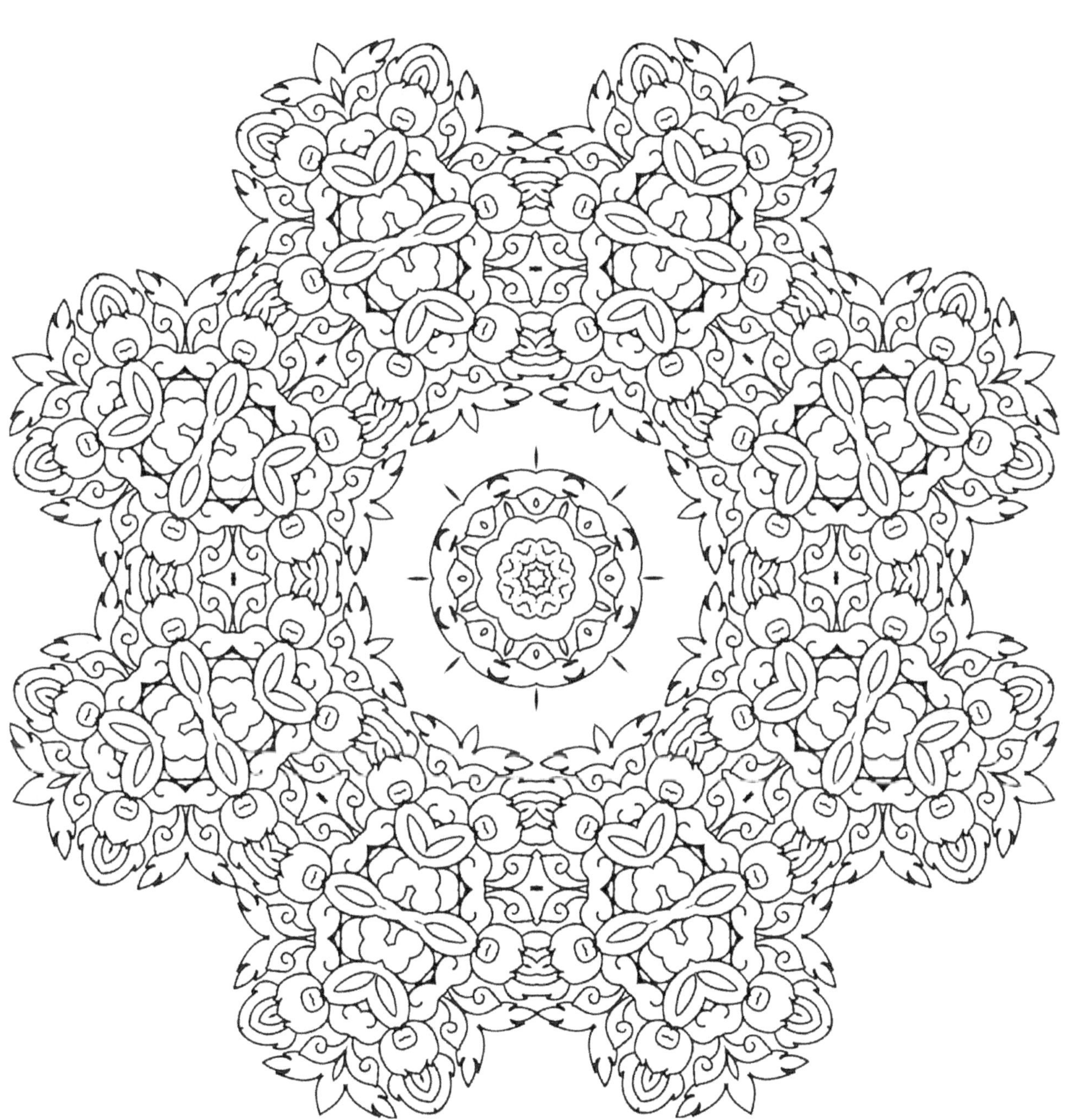

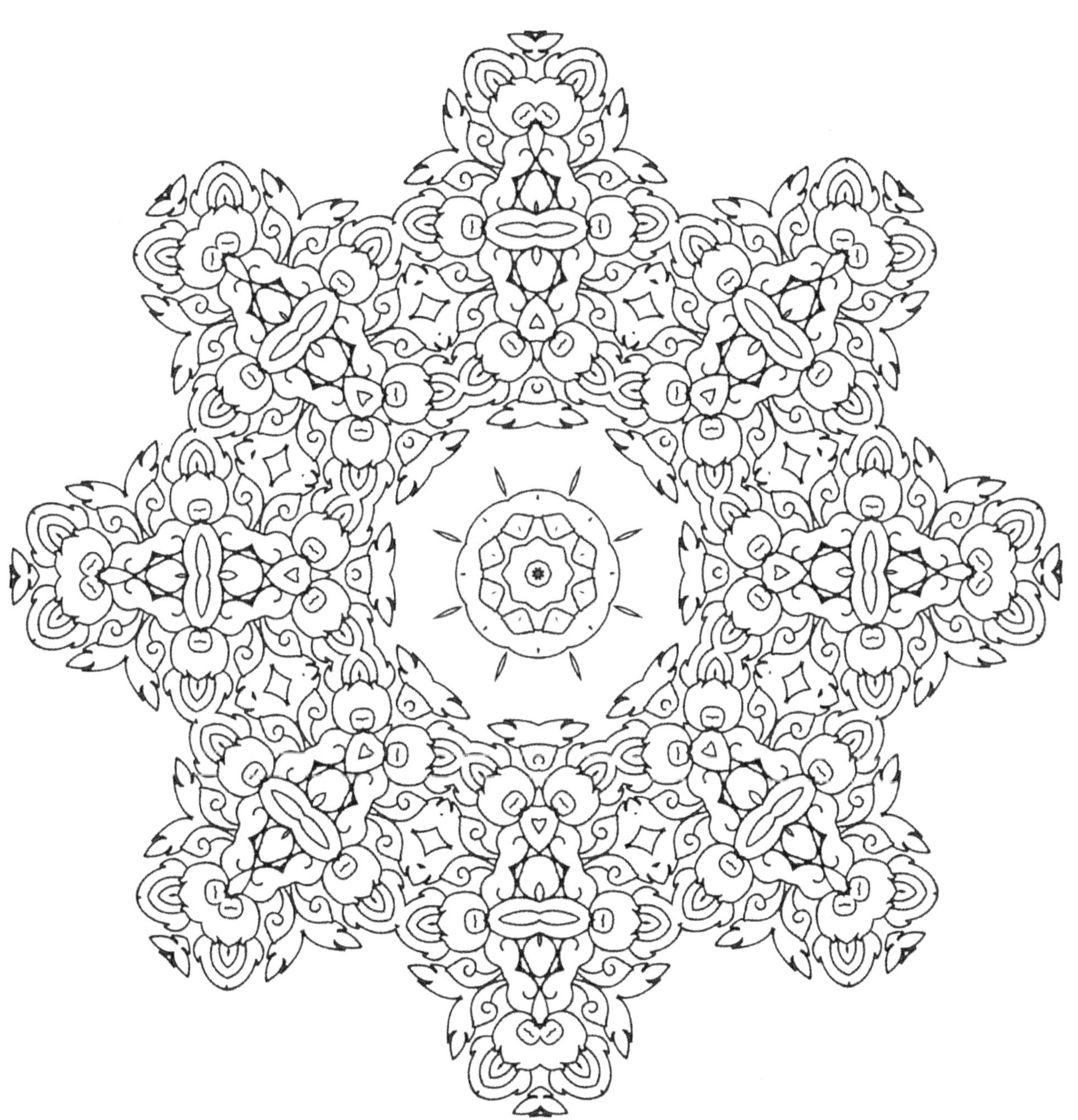

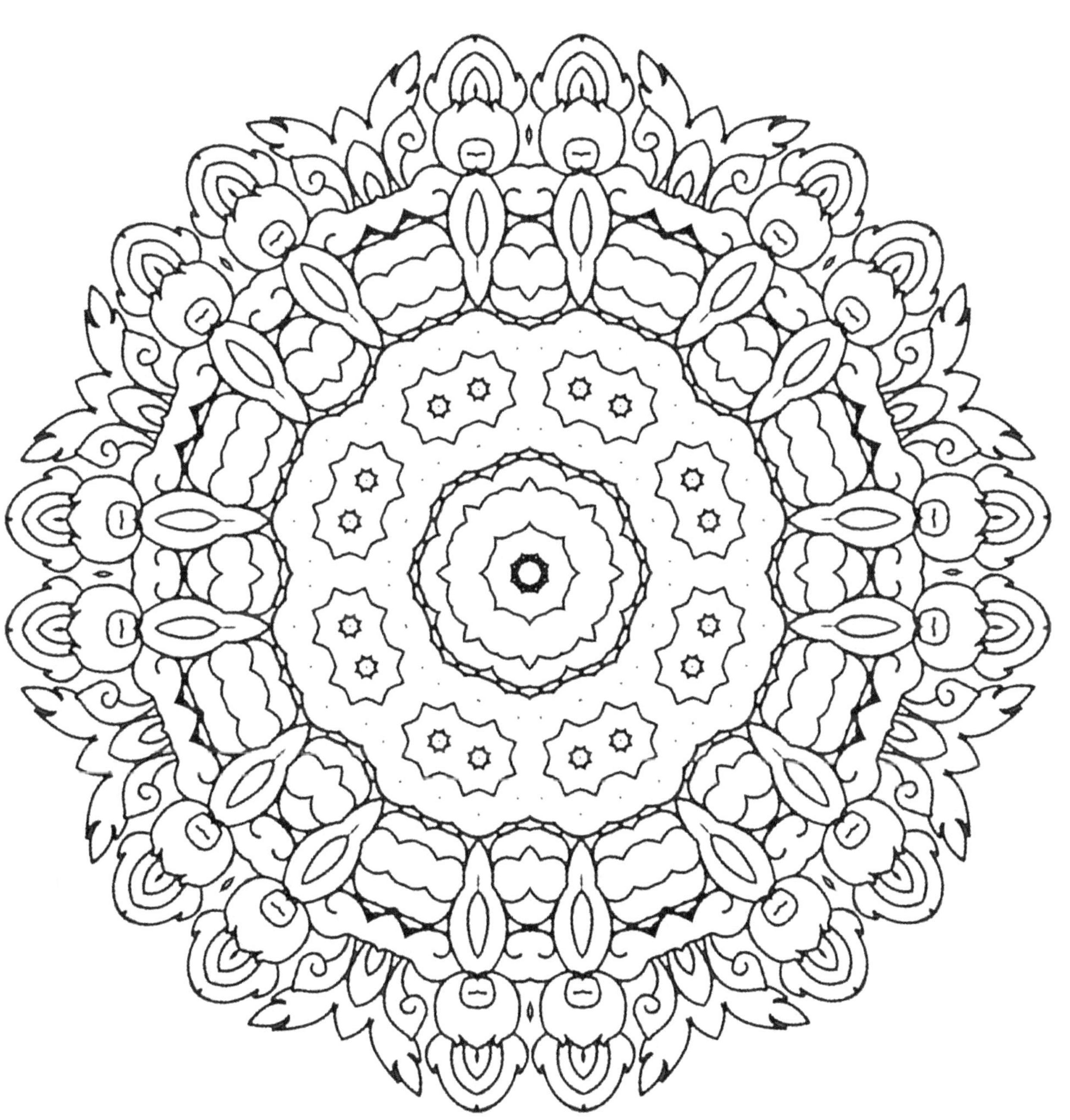

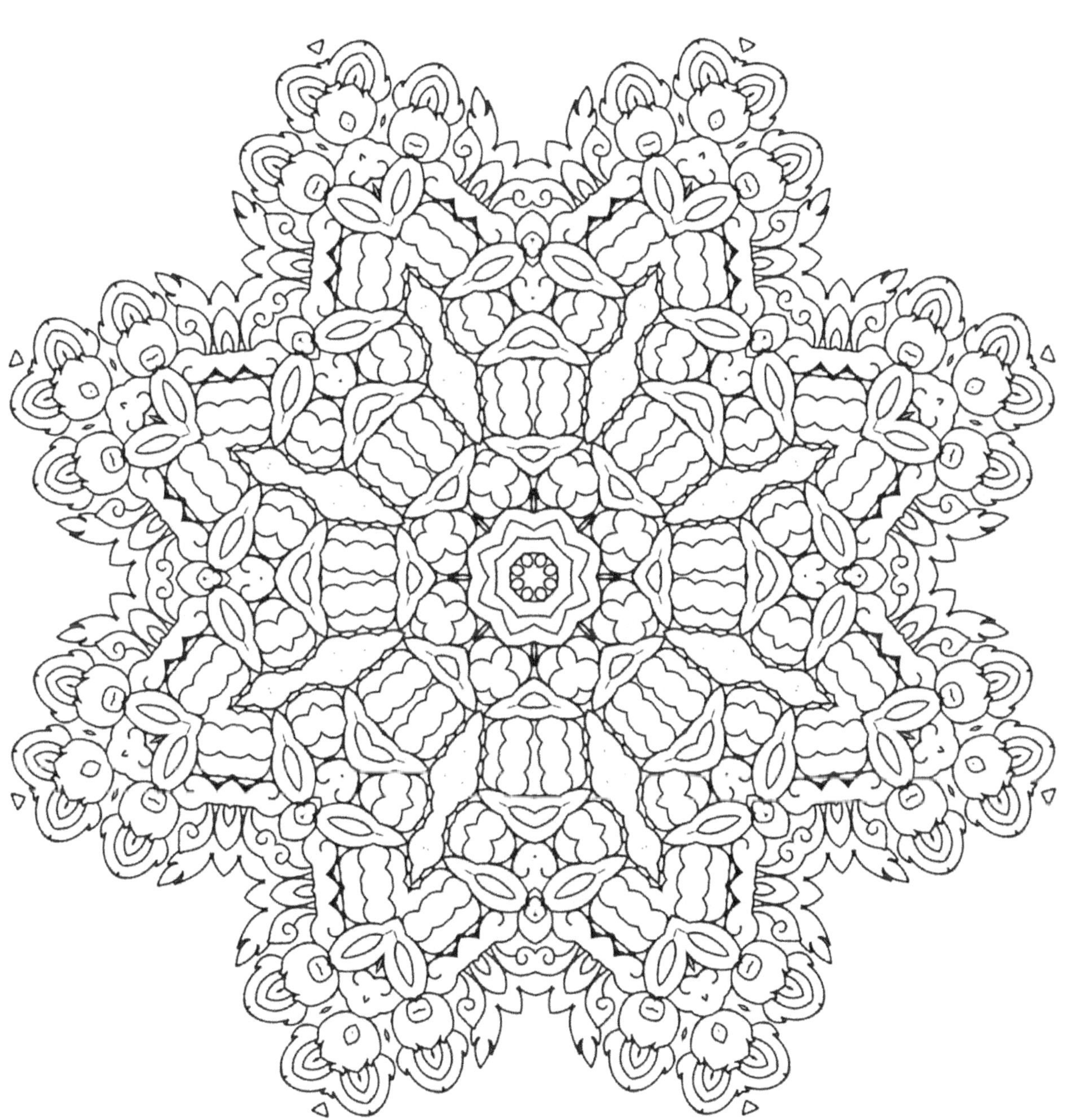

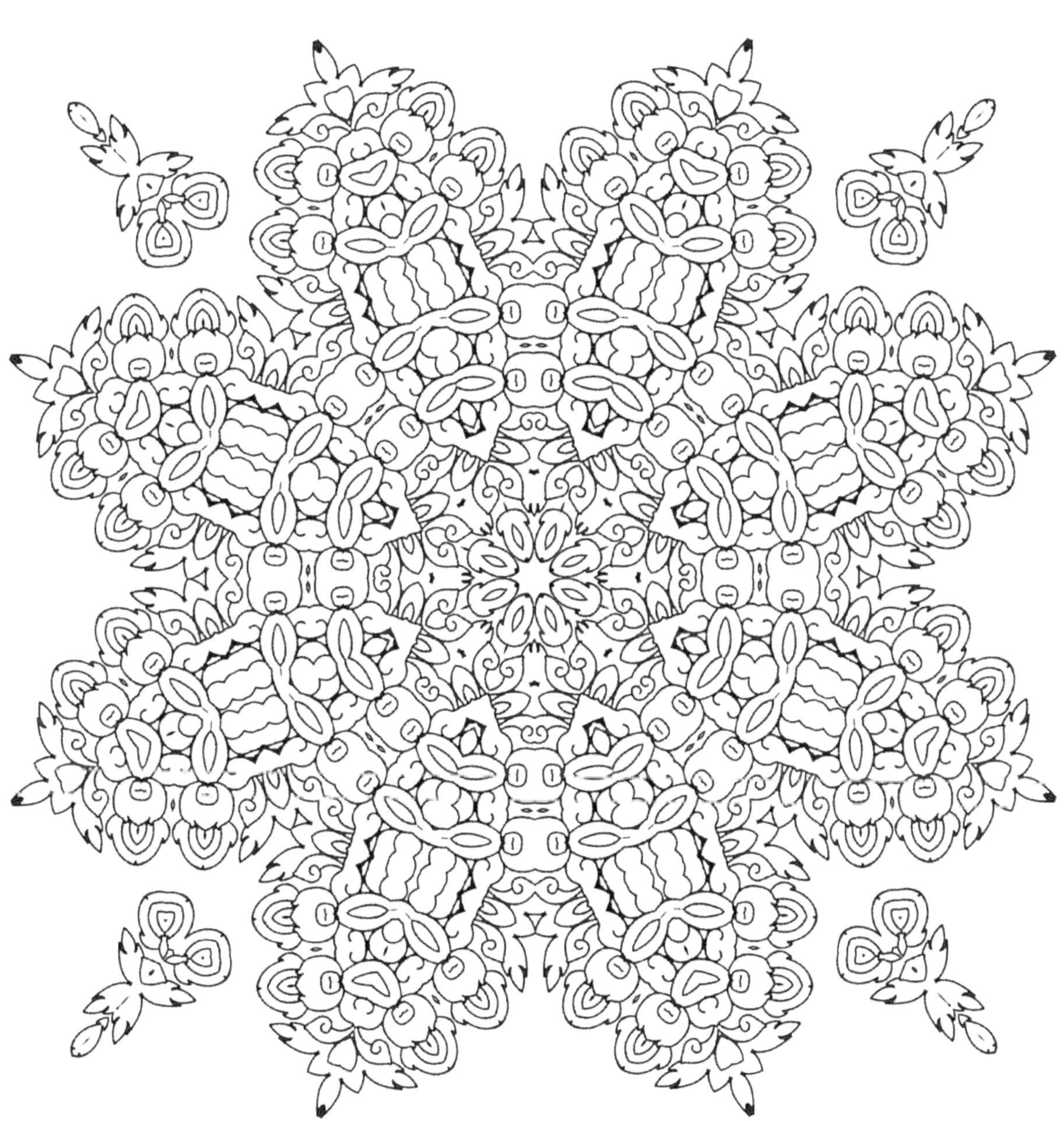

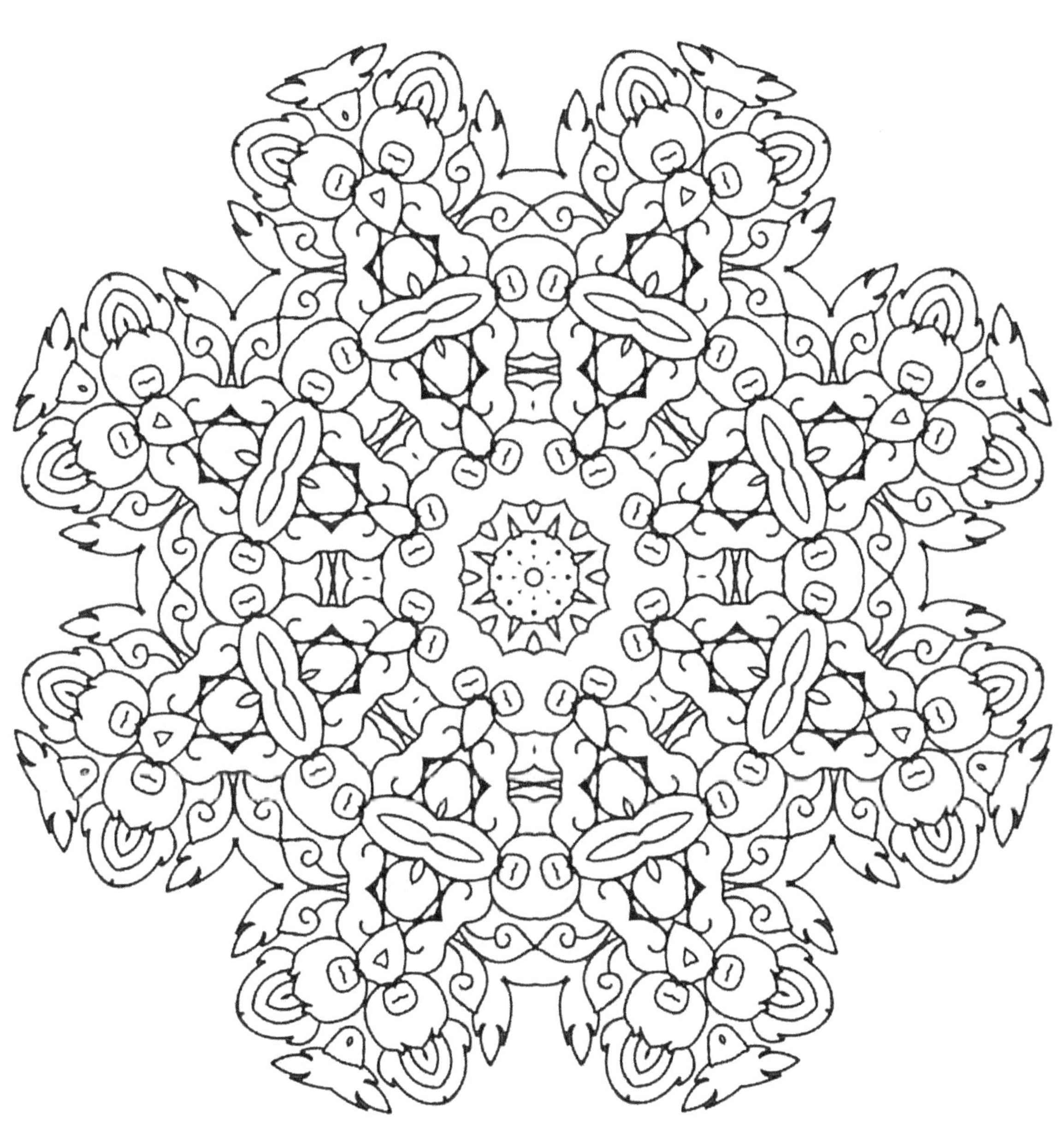

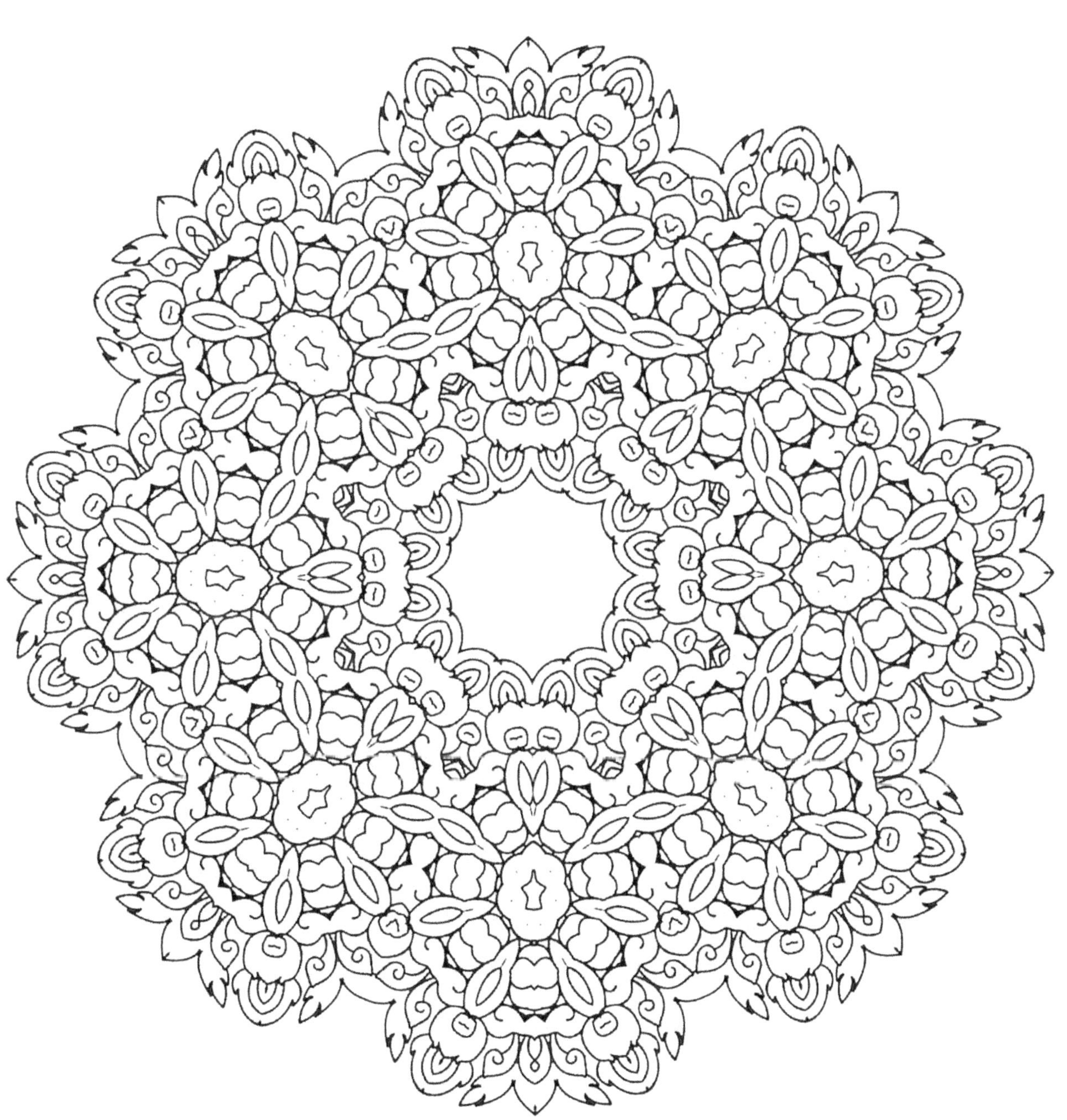

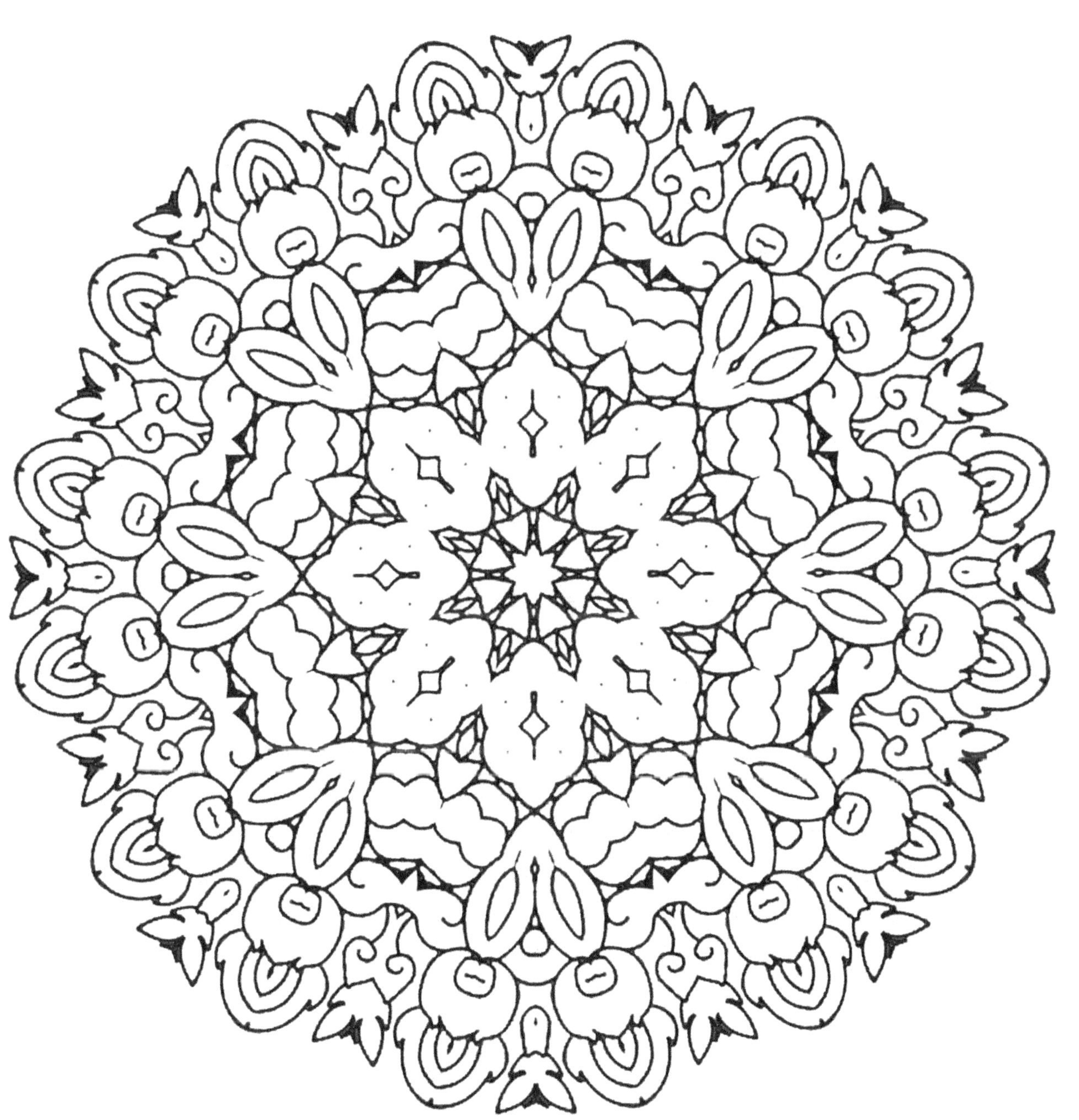

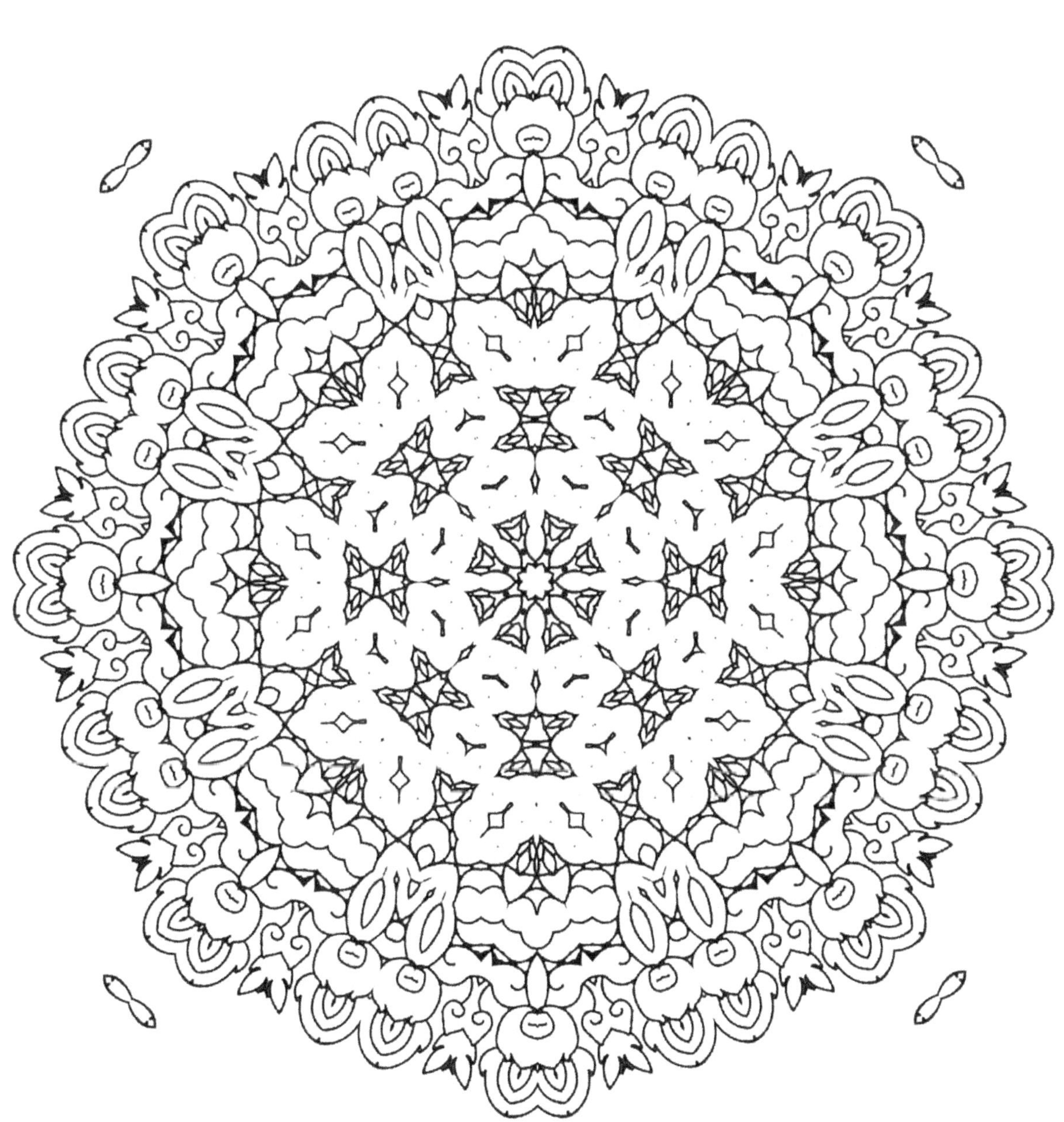

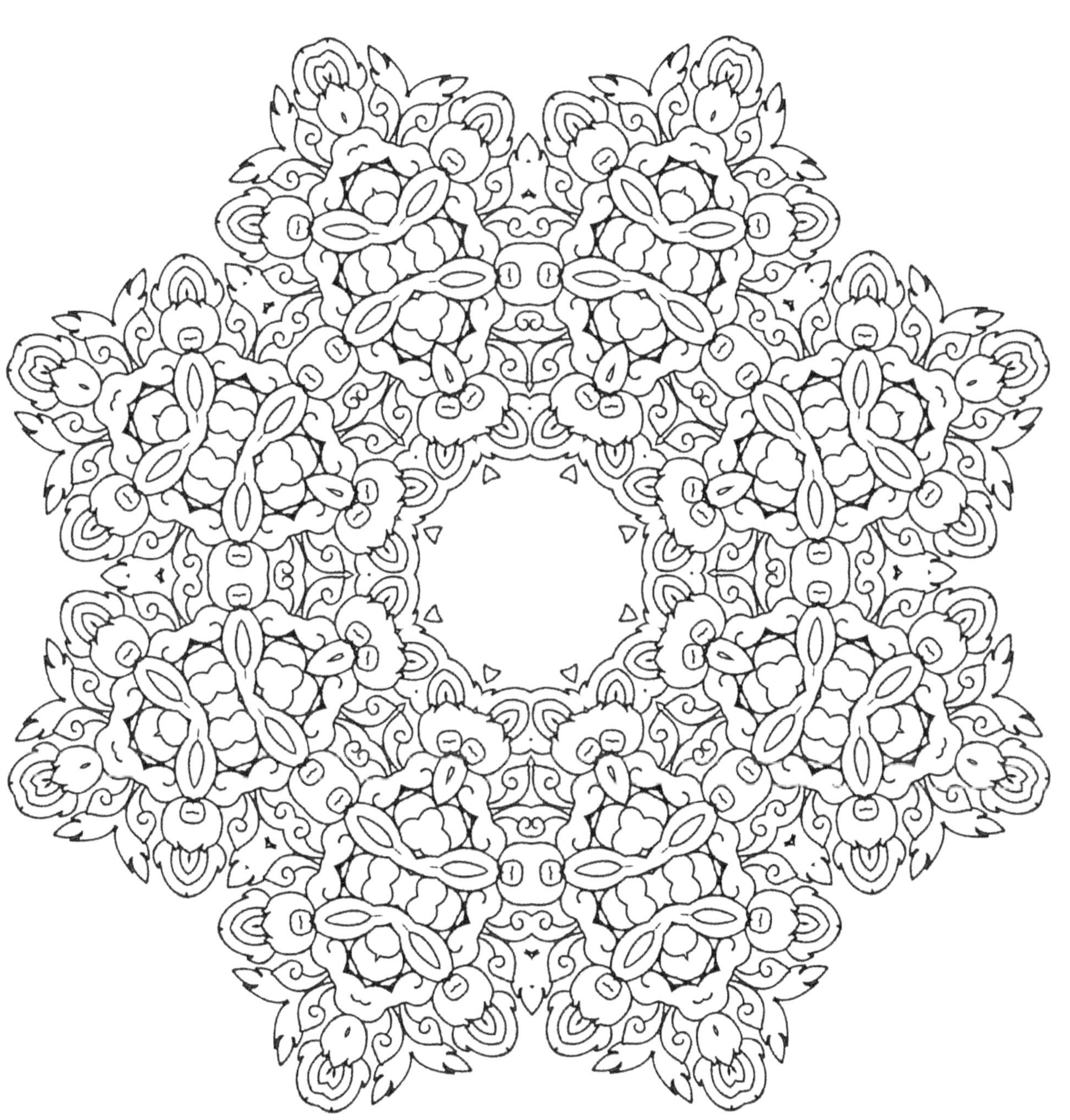

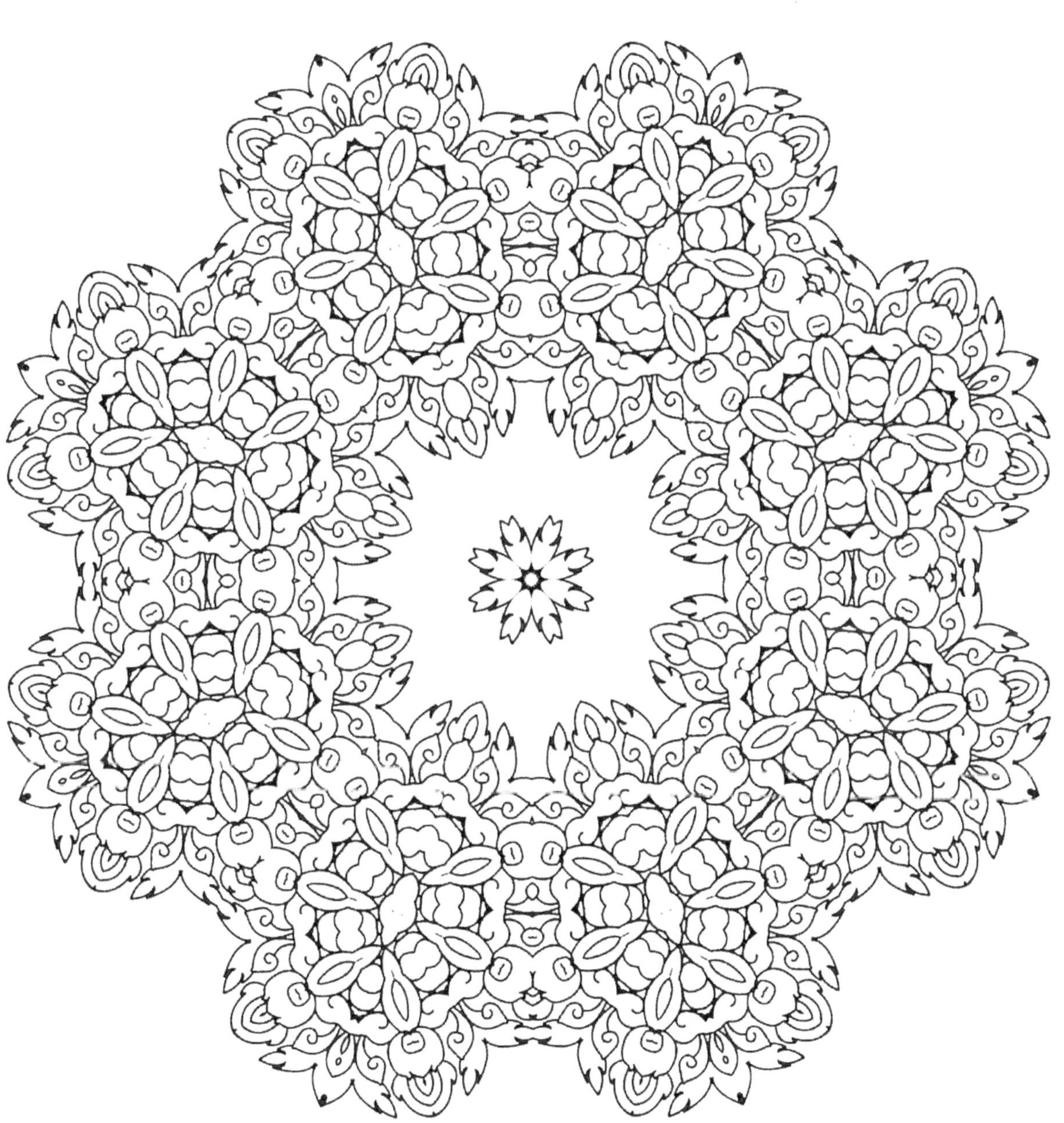

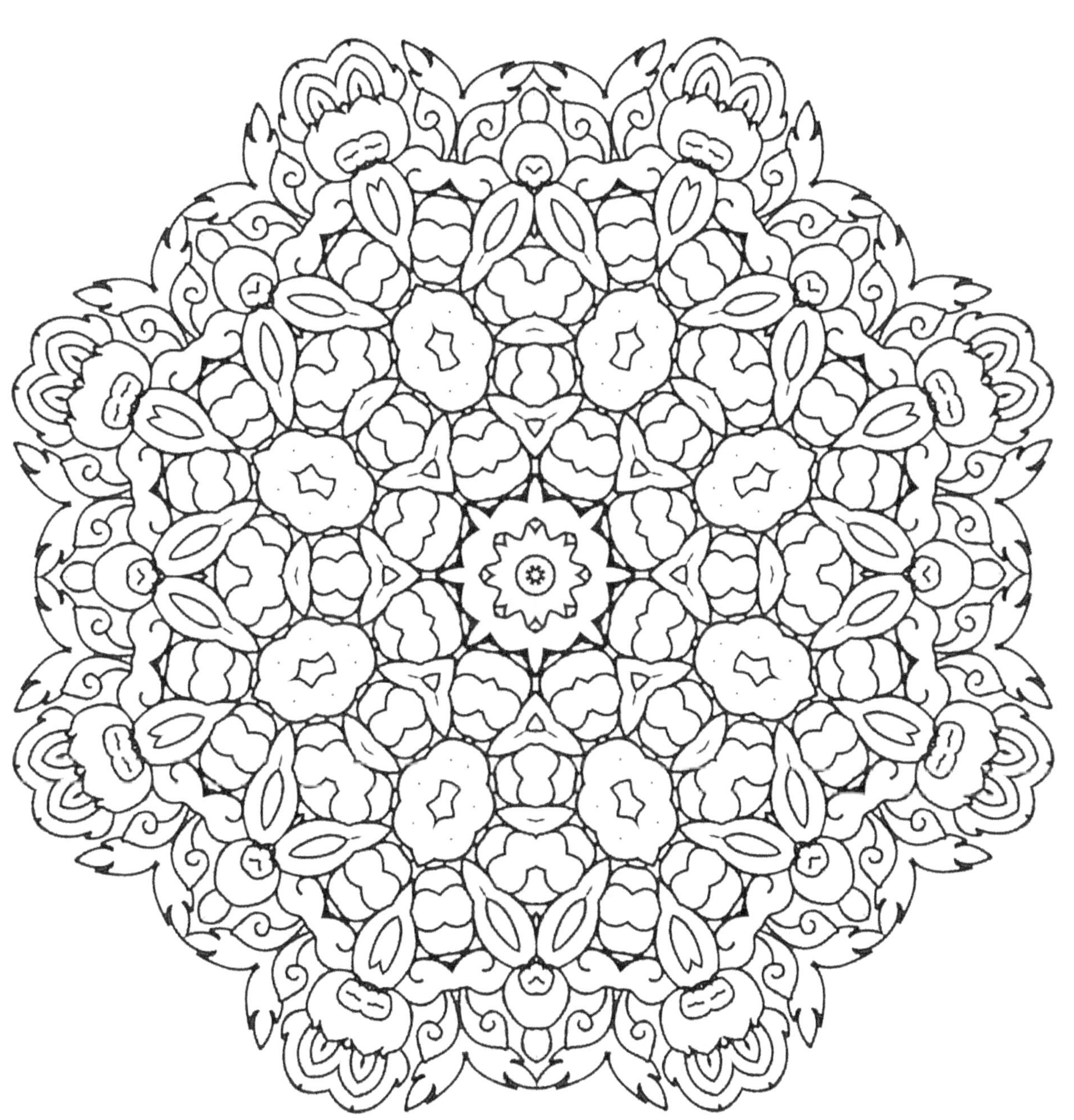

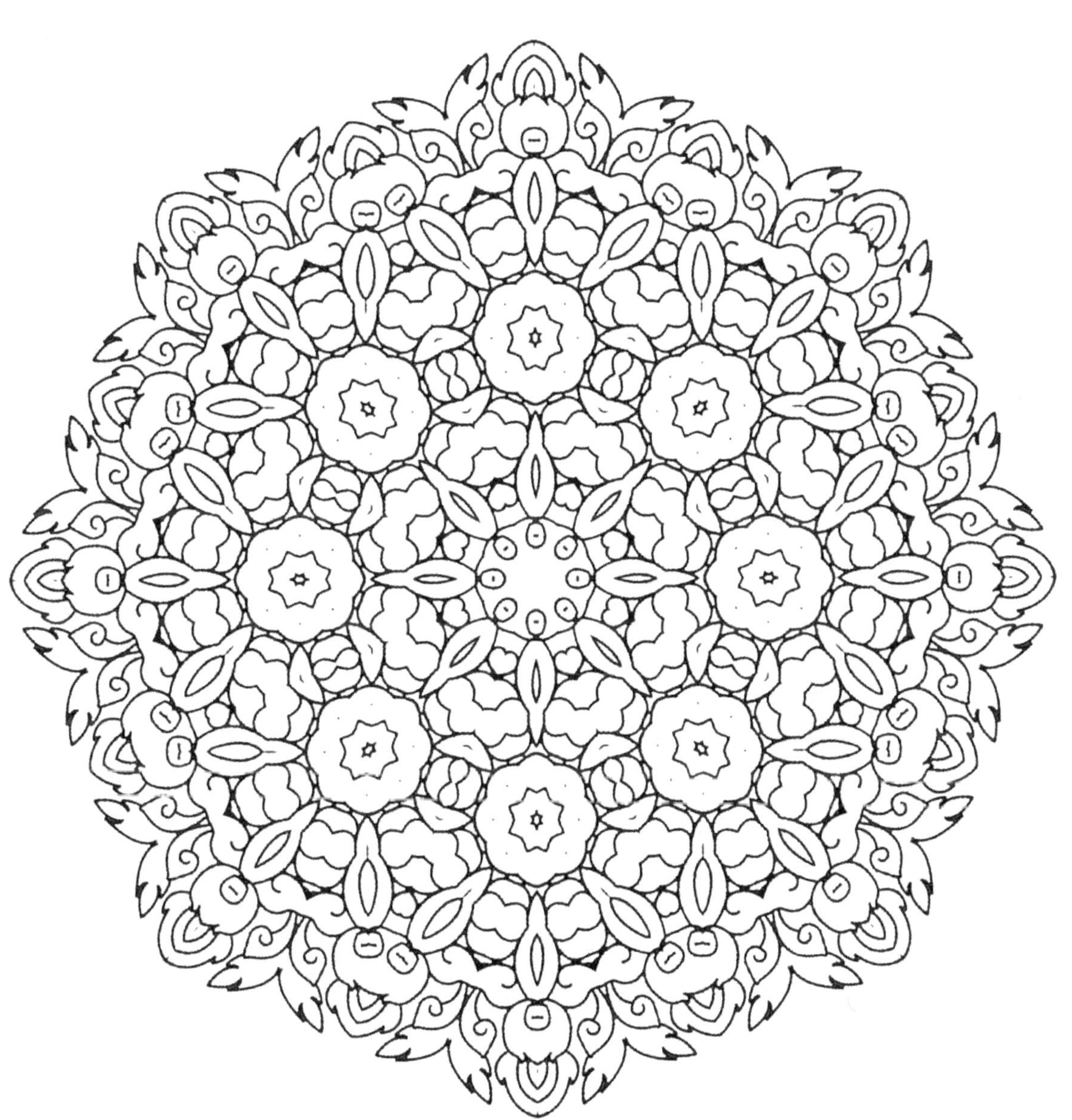

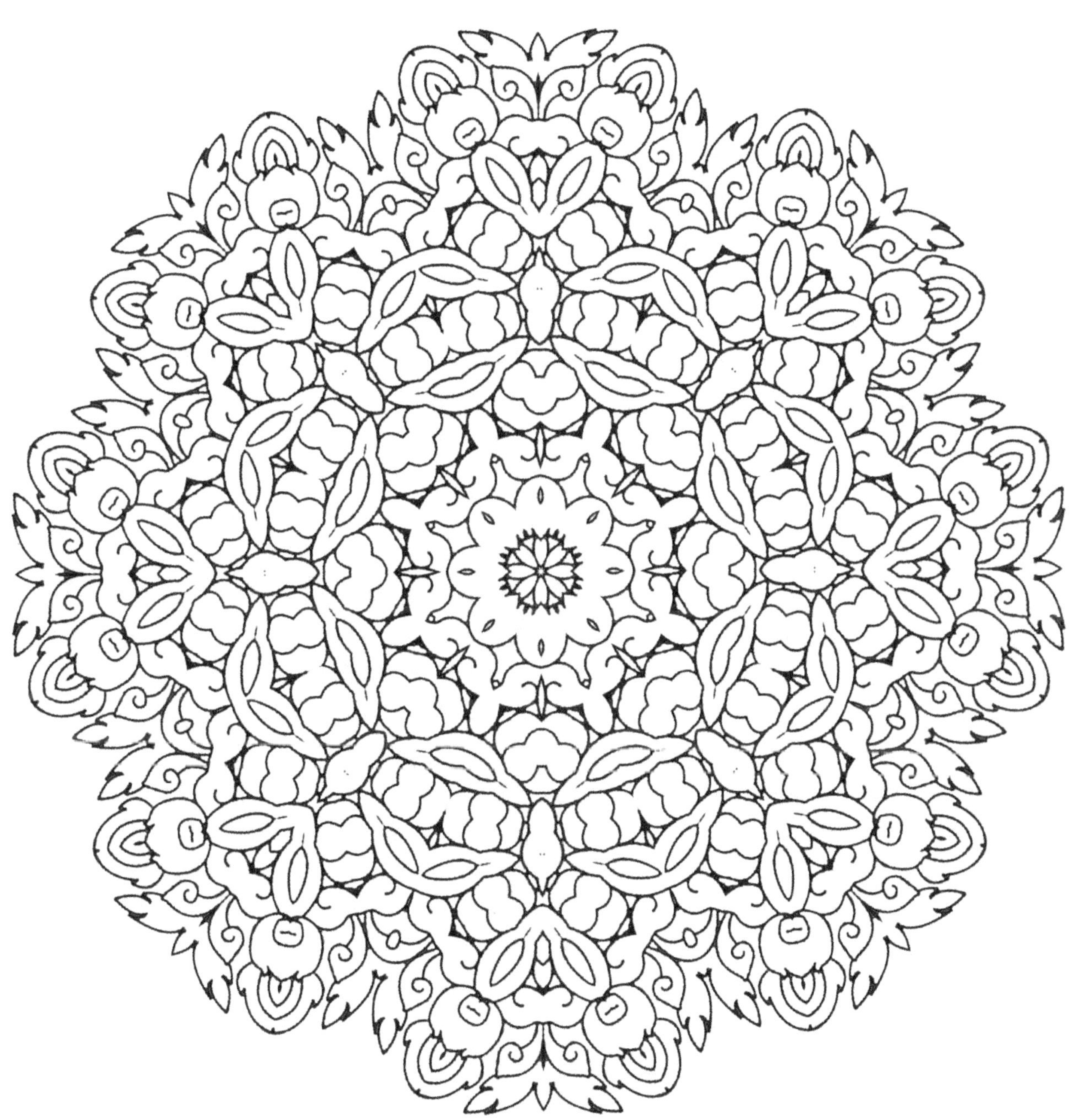

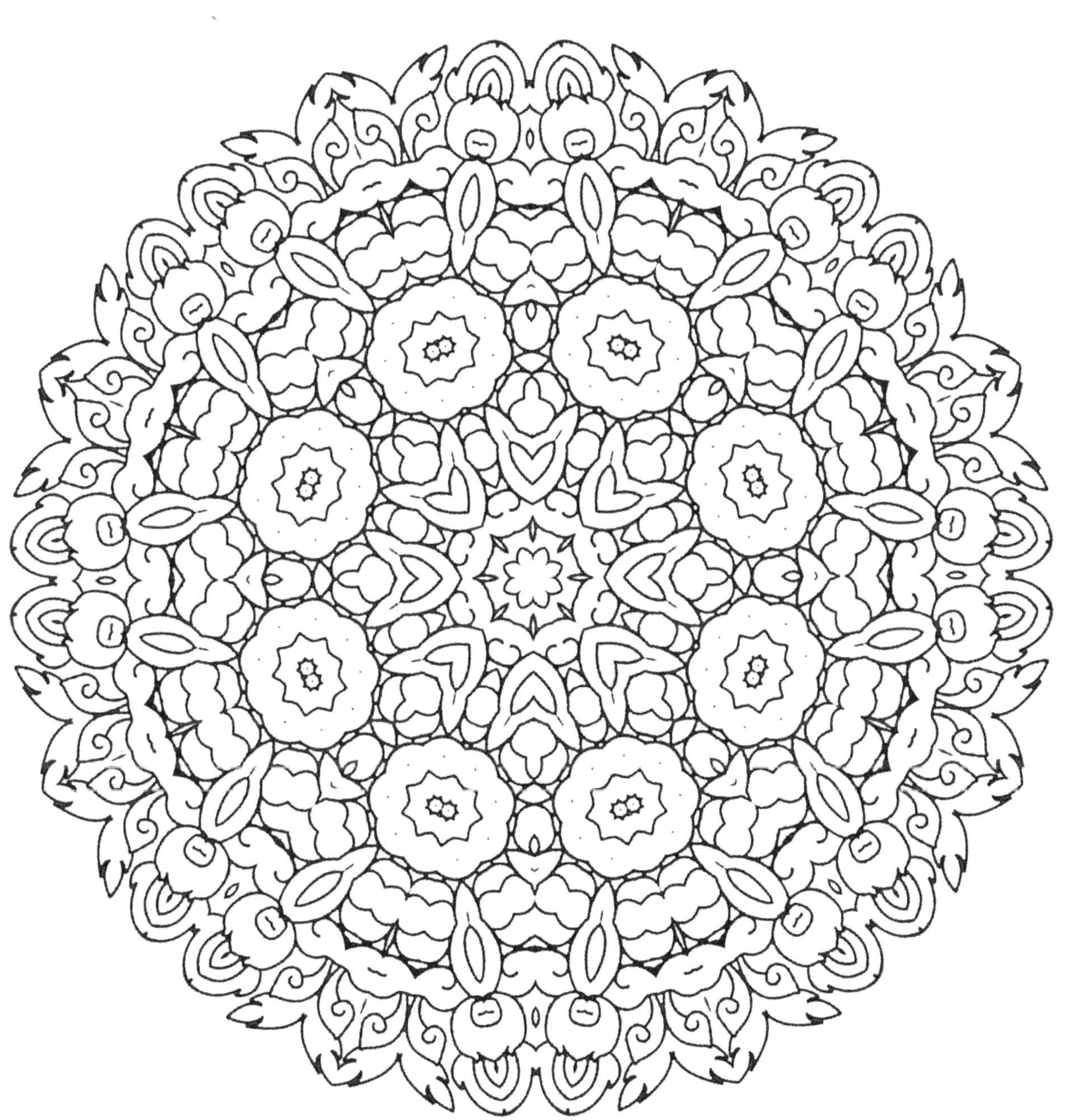

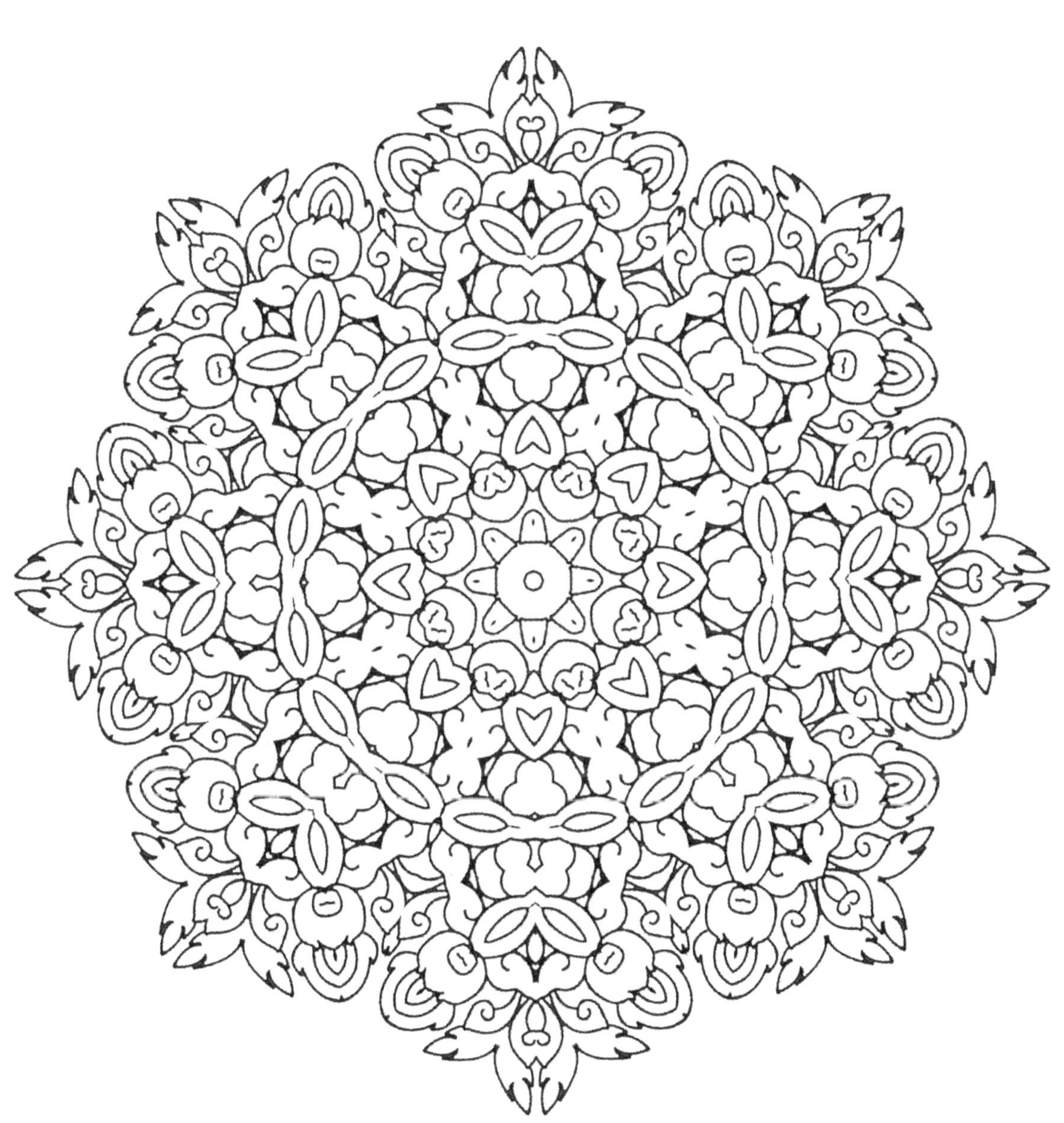

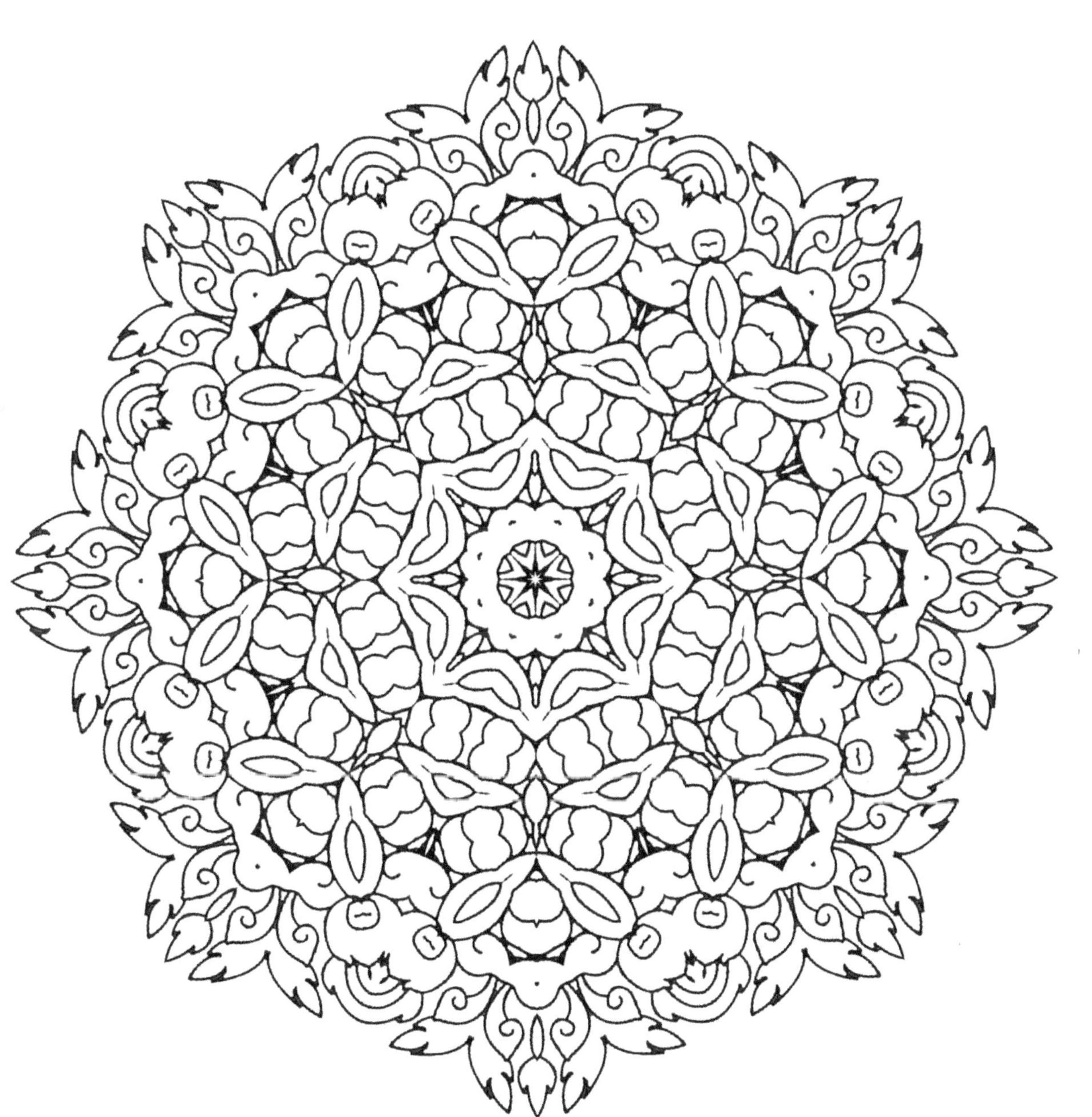

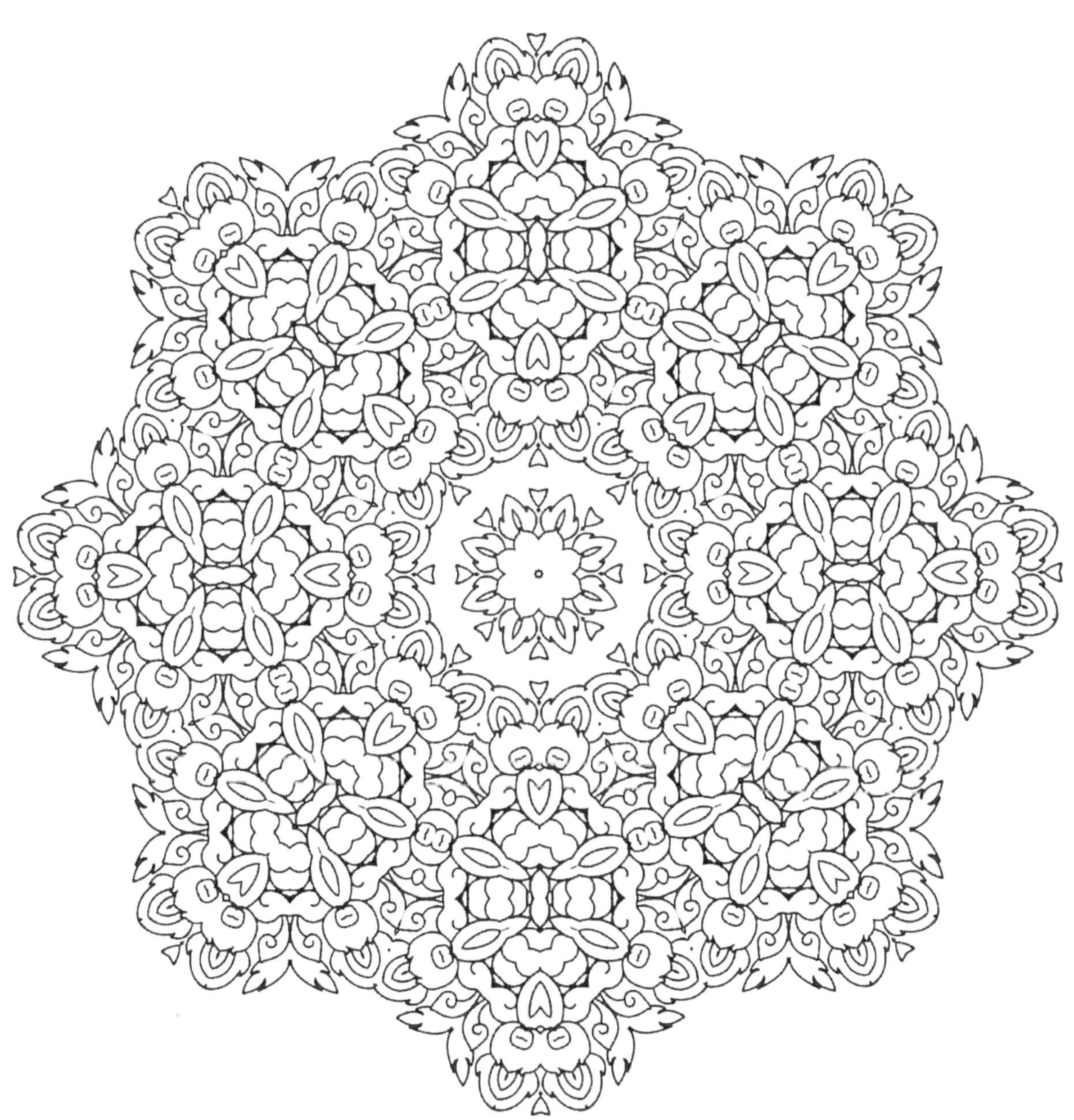

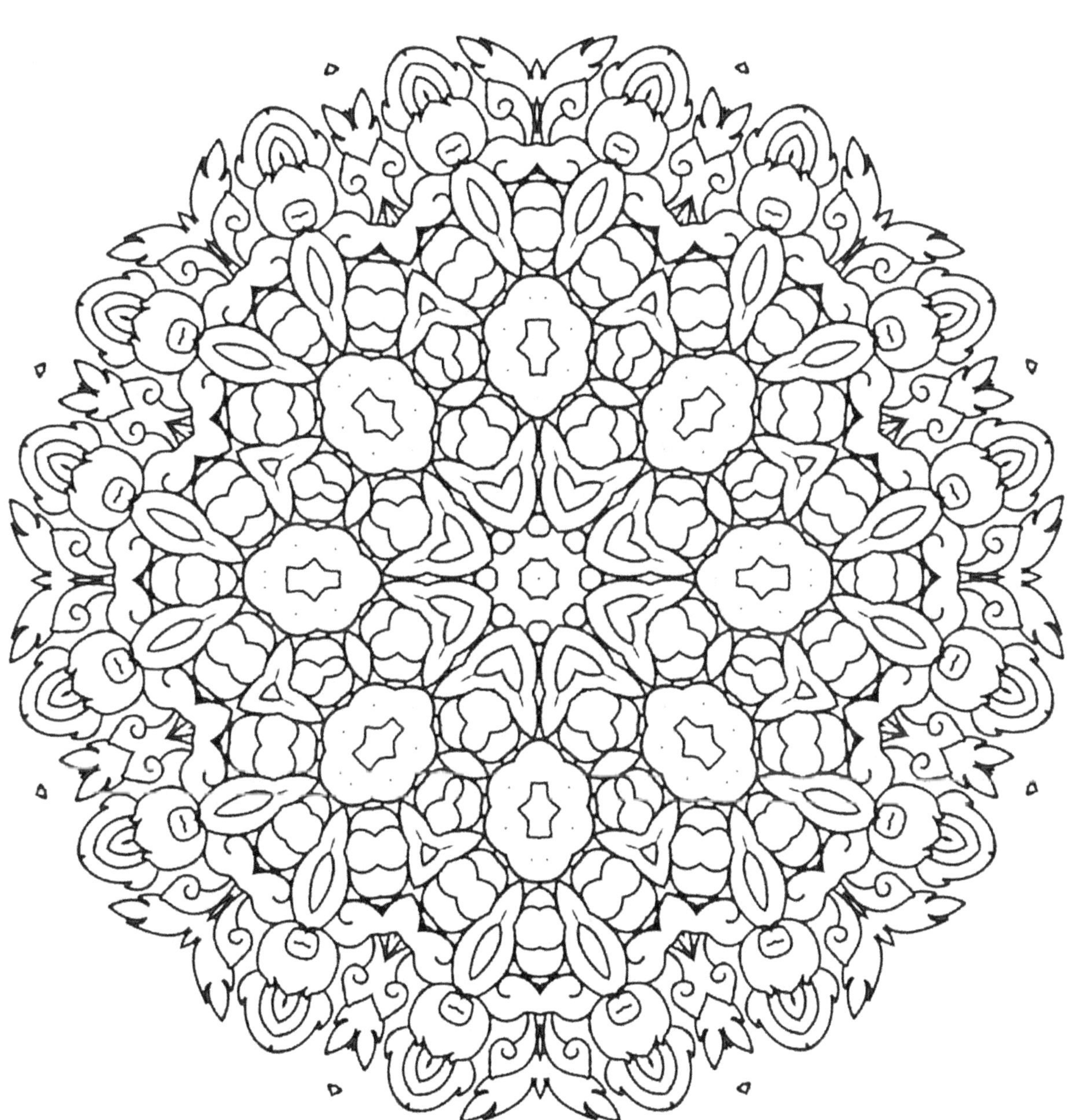

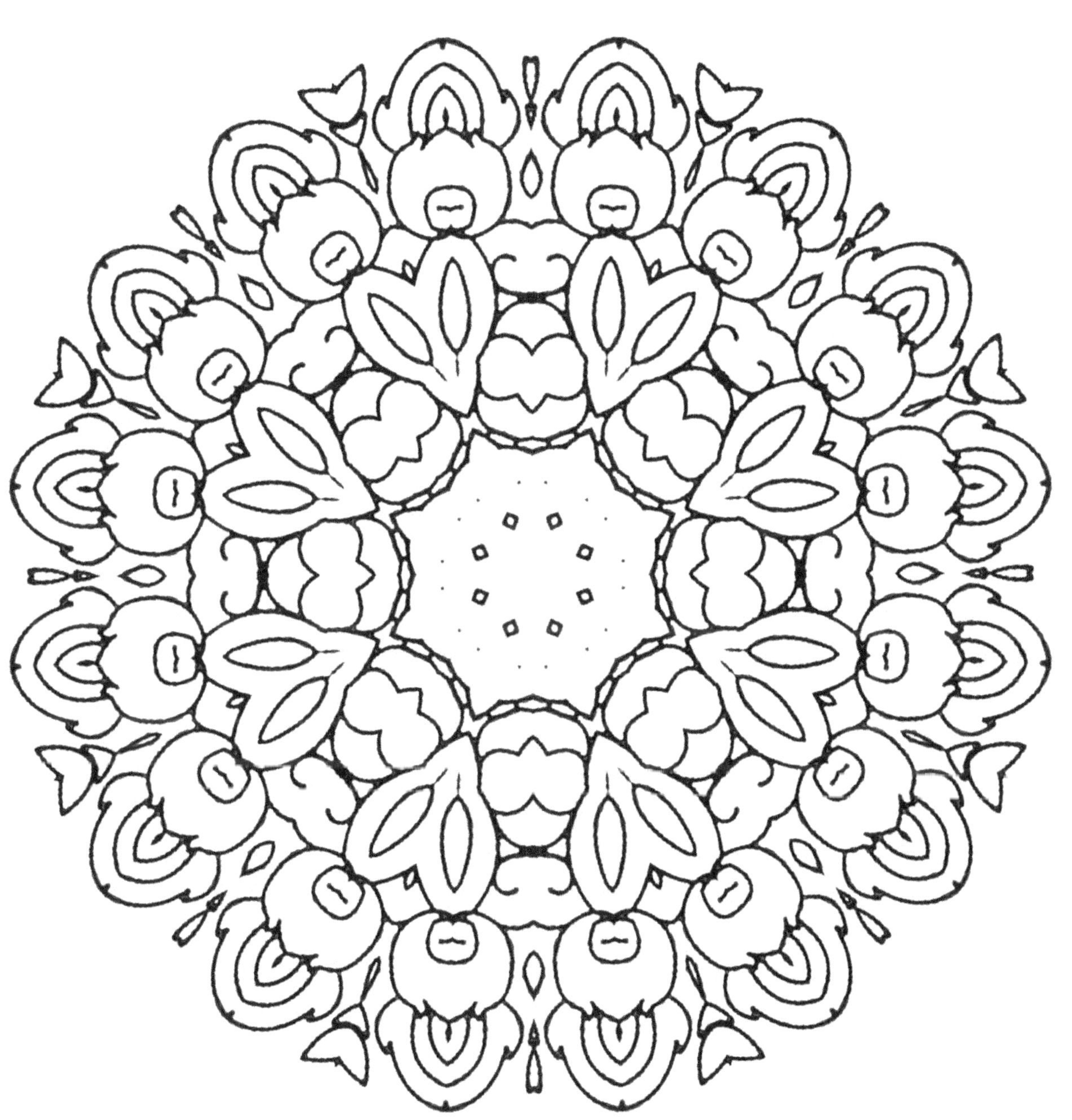

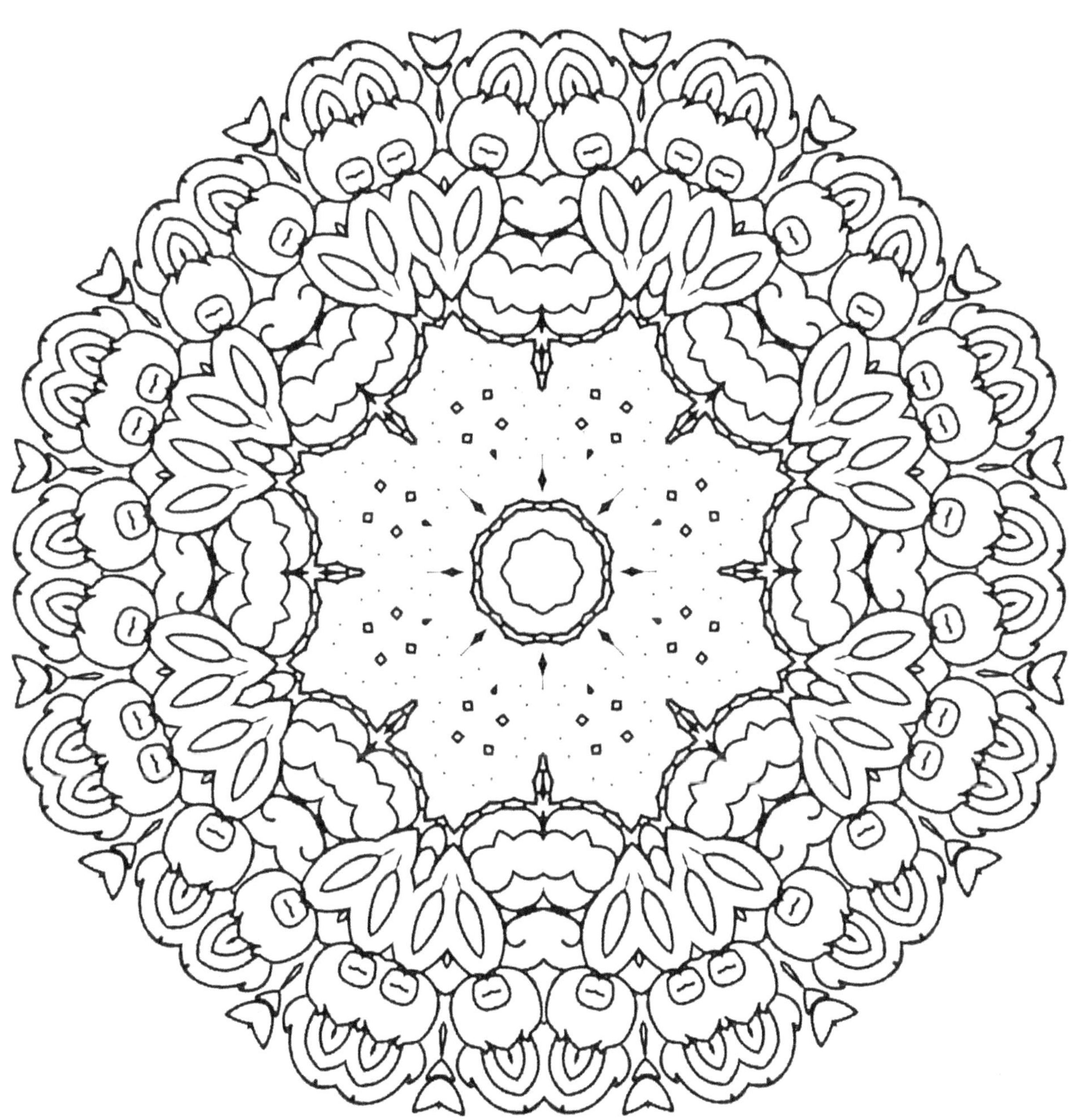

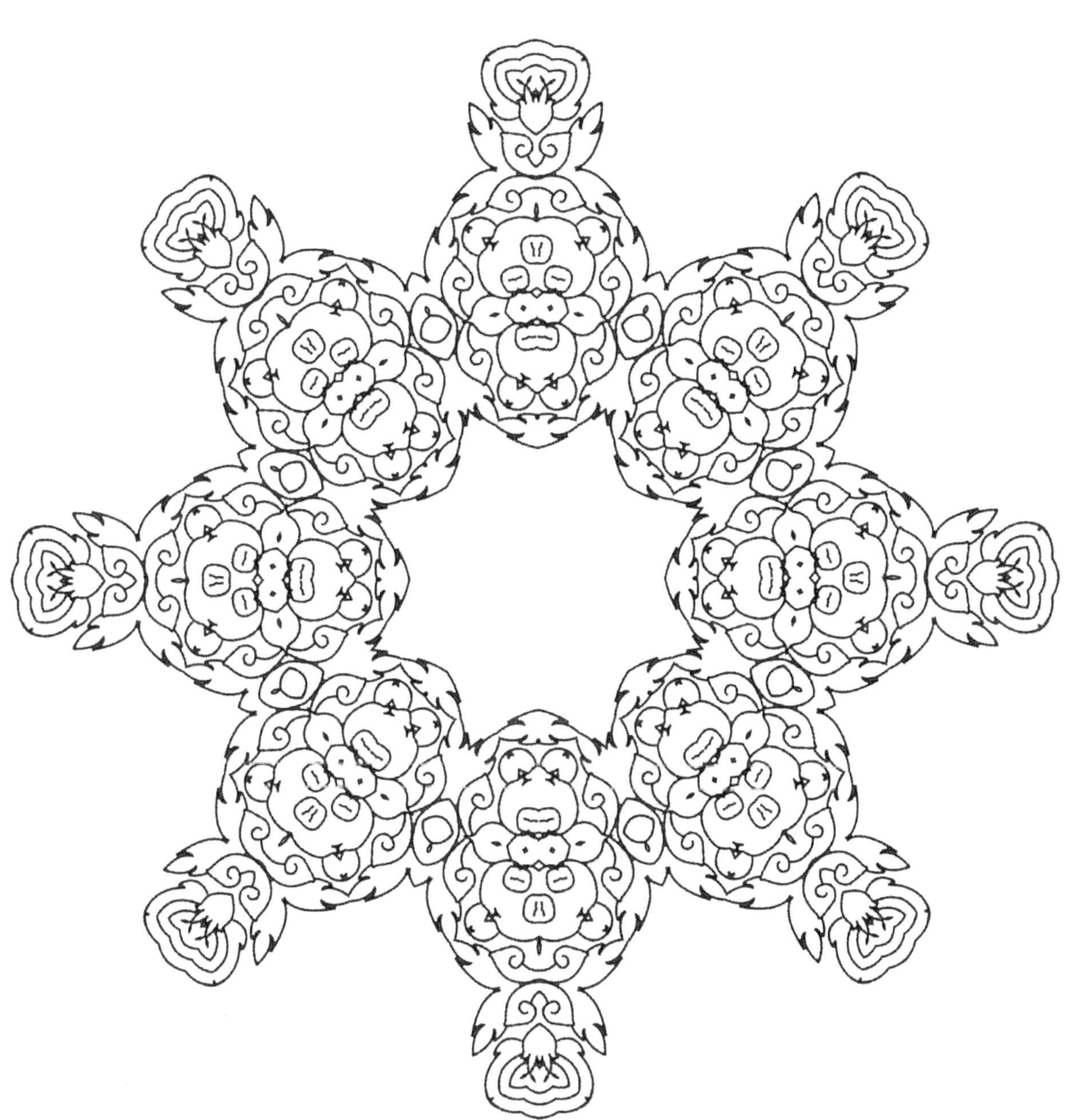

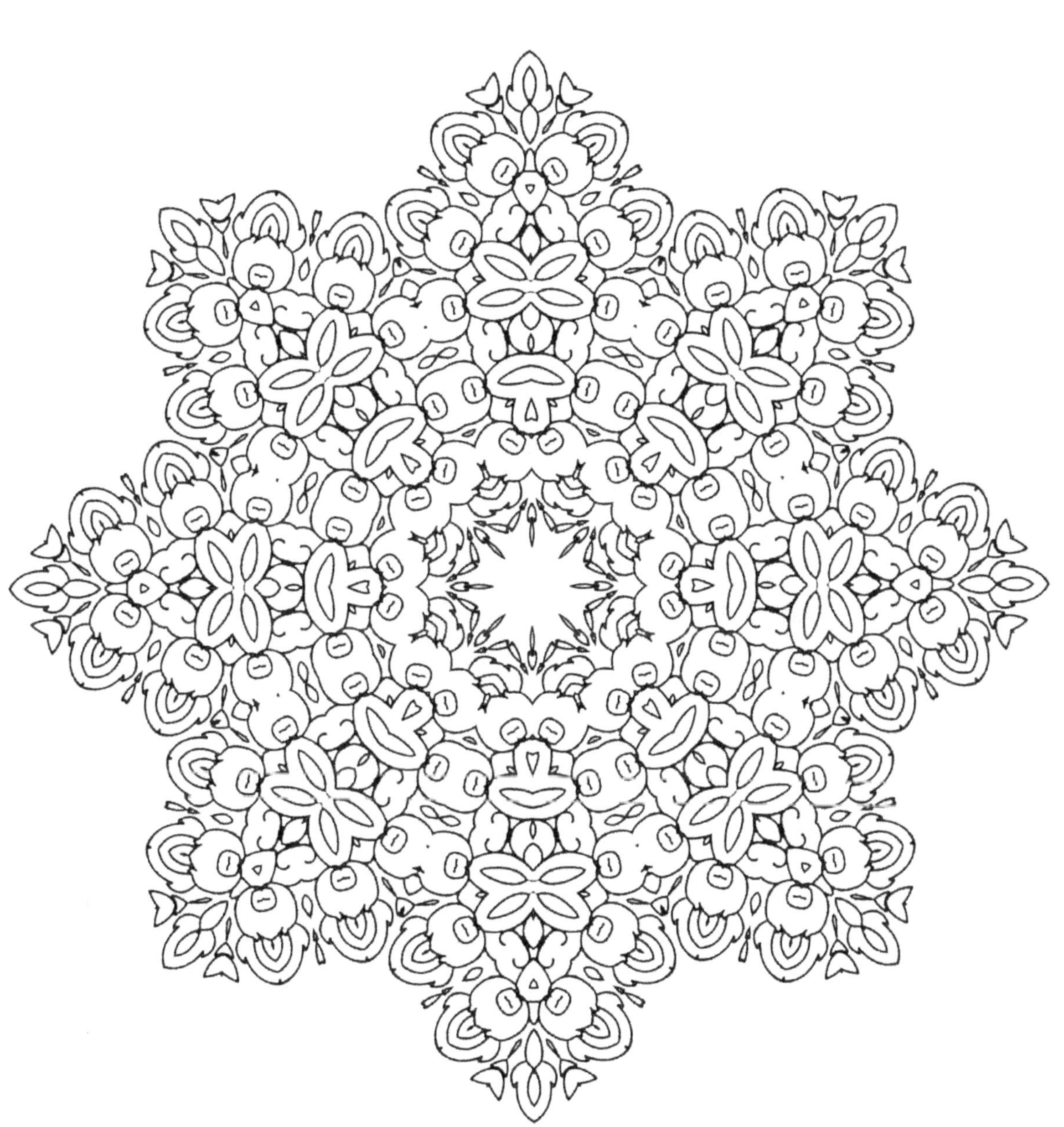

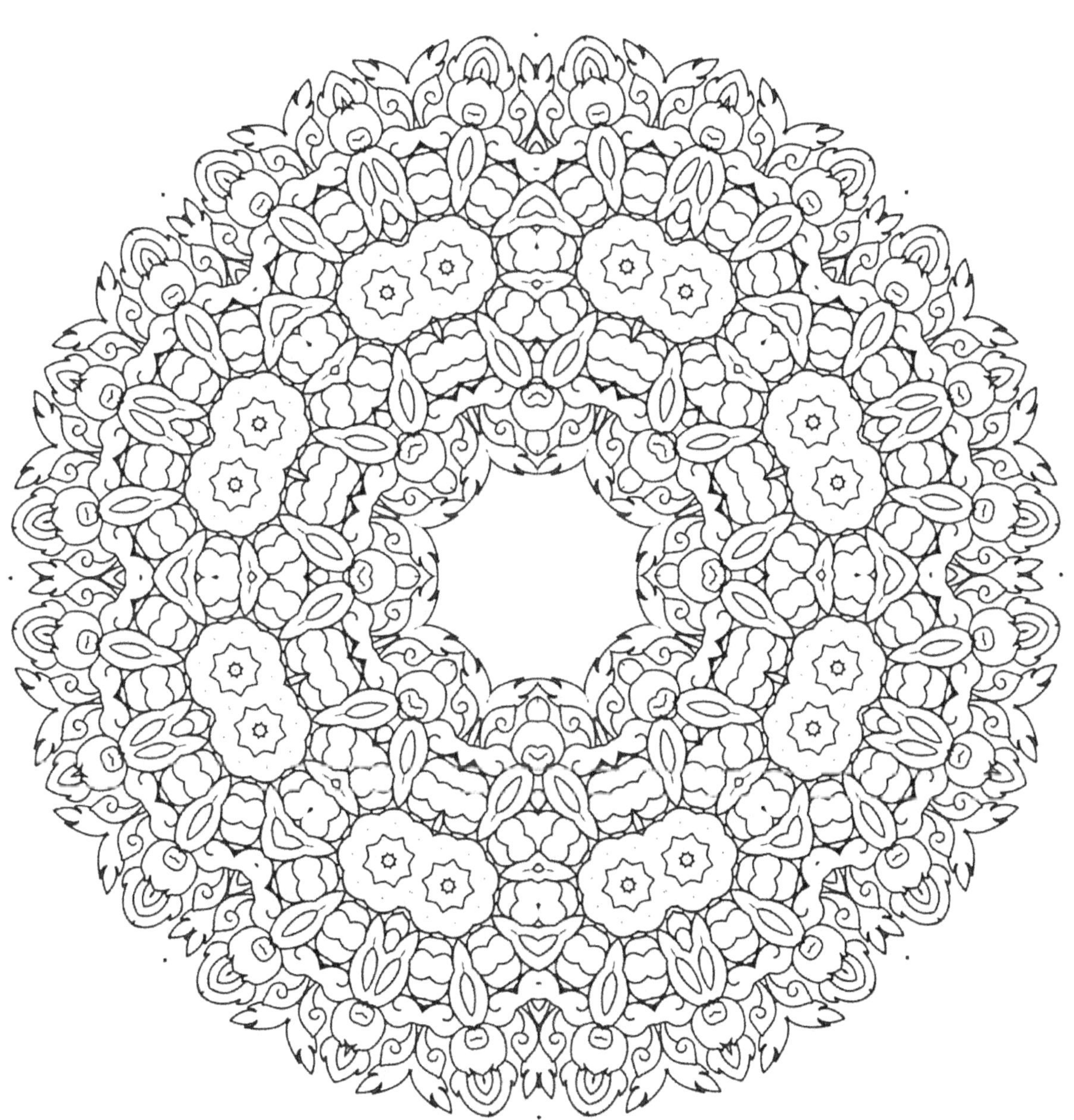

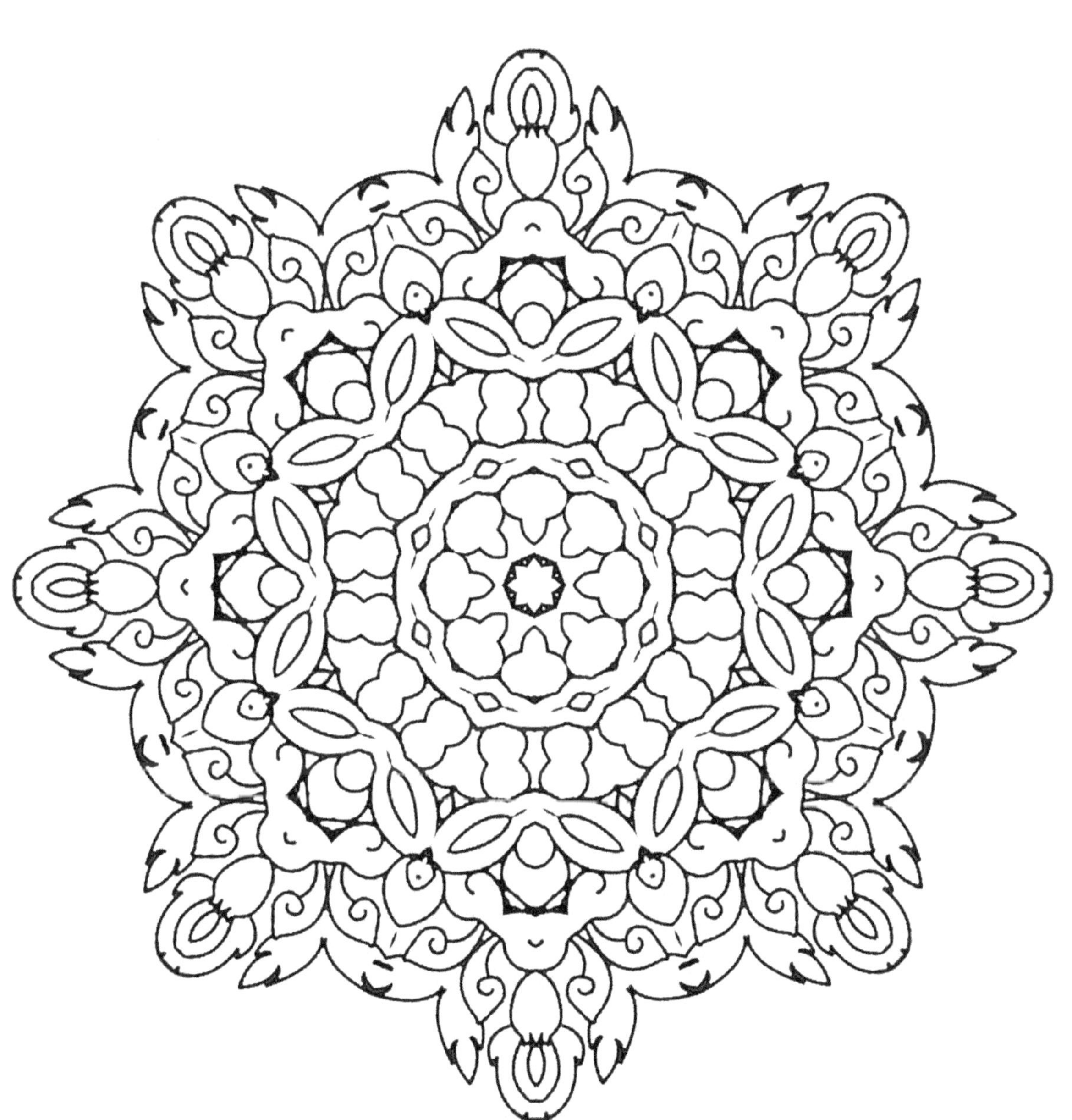

Thank you

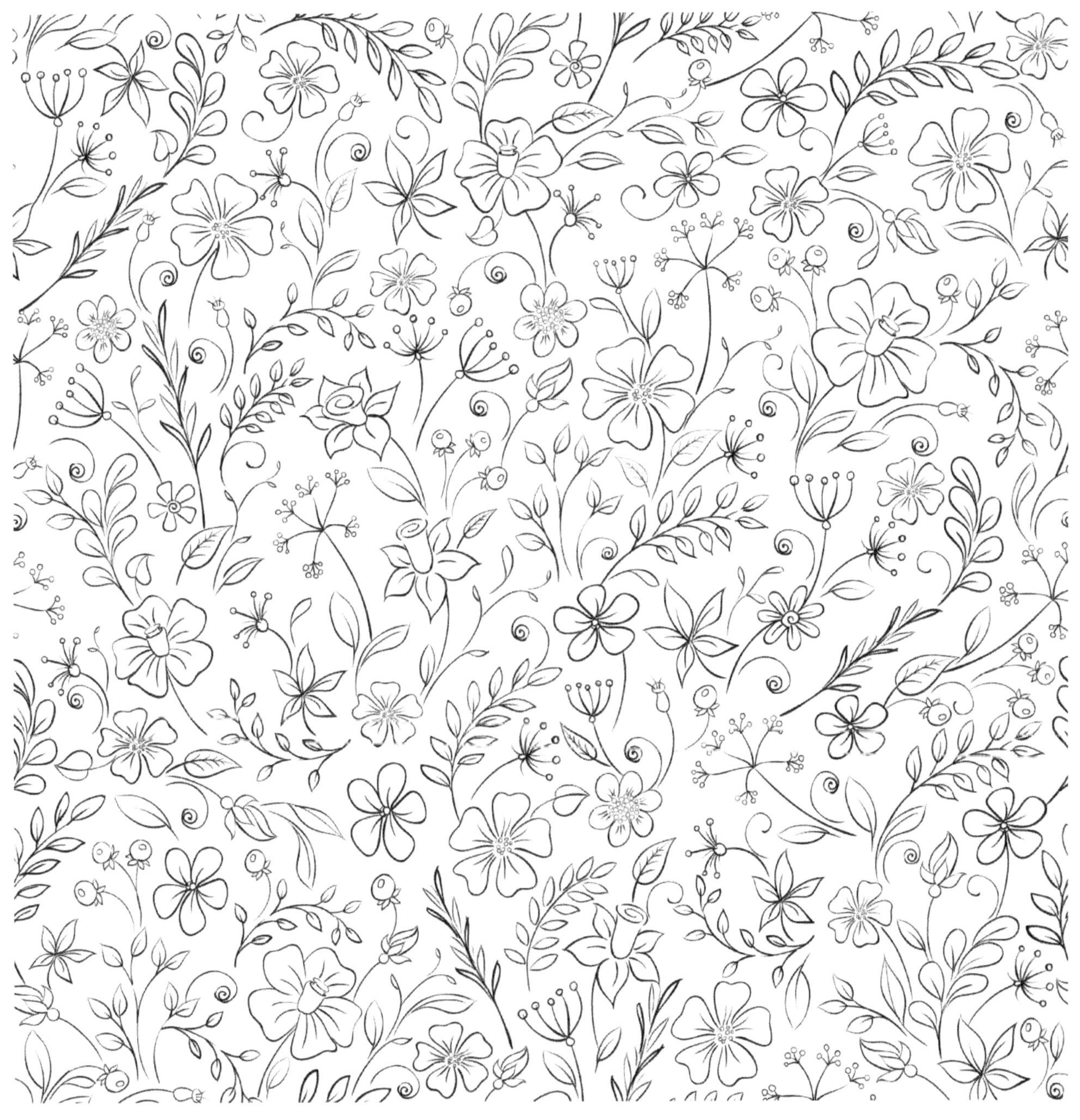

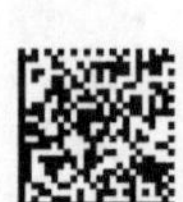